to doreen cleman—

please know i love
you— a i

thank God for
putting you in my life—

never give up!

gal. 2:20

Seduced
by
Success

Ann Kiemel Anderson

OLIVER
NELSON

THOMAS NELSON PUBLISHERS
Nashville

Published in Nashville, Tennessee, by Thomas Nelson, Inc.

Scripture quotations are from the *Holy Bible,* New Living
Translation, copyright © 1996. Used by permission of
Tyndale House Publishers, Inc., Wheaton, Illinois 60189.
All rights reserved.

Library of Congress Cataloging-in-Publication Data

Anderson, Ann Kiemel.
    Seduced by success / Ann Kiemel Anderson.
        p.   cm.
    ISBN 0-7852-7076-0 (hc.)
    1. Anderson, Ann Kiemel. 2. Christian biography—
United States. I. Title.
BR1725.A727A3   1998
277.3'0825'092—dc21
[b]   98-27232
                                                                CIP

Printed in the United States of America

1 2 3 4 5 6 7 BVG 04 03 02 01 00 99 98

To Doug Gill, M.D.
and
Herb and Dona Fisher

Without them I could never
have written this story.

Acknowledgments

I am so indebted to Peggy Schulze, a Moms In Touch partner, who typed this manuscript with love.

Victor Oliver has been a part of my publishing books for twenty-plus years. There is no one I respect more in this arena.

Cindy Blades, editor at Thomas Nelson, has been outstanding at making sure my thoughts are integrated.

My sister, Jan, has been there to help me with every book I've ever written . . . including this one. She deserves her name somewhere on every book cover.

With *special* love to her son, Christian Anderson Ream, my nephew. He is two months younger than Taylor, my firstborn, and full of magic and potential. He has blessed me and shared so much of his mother with me and my children.

To my husband, Will, and our four treasured sons. They are my life.

This has been very difficult to write, yet I told God there was *nothing* I would not do for Him if He would deliver me . . . set me free. God kept His end of the bargain, and writing this book is part of keeping my word with God.

Maybe there are many of you who have walked some of these roads too. May these pages give you hope . . . and remember, *nothing* is too hard for the God of the universe.

Though the LORD gave you adversity
for food and affliction for drink, he will
still be with you to teach you. You will
see your teacher with your own eyes,
and you will hear a voice say, "This is
the way; turn around and walk here."
Then you will destroy all your silver
idols and gold images. You will throw
them out like filthy rags. . . . Then the
LORD will bless you. . . . So it will be
when the LORD begins to heal his people
and cure the wounds he gave them.
(Isaiah 30:20–26)

Introduction

I am Ann.

I grew up in Hawaii in a parsonage. My father was an old-fashioned preacher who believed sin is real, God is good, and love transcends everything!

My mother was beautiful and smart and felt her mission was to assist my father and care for her children.

My brother, Fred, is almost six years older than my sister and I. Jan is my identical twin sister, and I felt it was my

mission in life to protect her and be her
leader.

After graduating from college, I did some
graduate work in journalism and was offered
enviable job opportunities. A publisher
approached me and talked me into writing a
book. Though a total unknown in the
publishing world, my simple book, *I'm Out to
Change My World*, became a best-seller, as did
my next book, *I Love the Word Impossible*. In
fact, at one point, I had five books in the top
ten!

I ran and trained for marathons, qualifying
for three Bostons, and ran many other
26.2-mile courses, even in Israel.

At thirty-five, I married Will Anderson and
moved from Boston to Idaho where my
husband had a large seed potato ranch. After
multiple miscarriages, God miraculously
blessed us with four beautiful sons through
open adoption. I was each birth mother's
labor coach, and Will and I witnessed each
one's incredible birth.

Behind all the accomplishments and radiant, stellar performances lived my gouging heart of pain. Somehow I believed that if I could be smart enough and find some gushing notoriety, I would finally become whole and complete. But nothing was enough. I was insatiable. Driven.

Today I understand that I was never enough before best-selling books and standing ovations. Thus I was not enough with them. External glory does not equate with a peaceful, integrated, healthy, and whole life.

Thus it is a glorious thing when God sets someone free. I know because He did this for me.

Free from myself. From my self-loathing and gaping insecurities.

Two years ago I stood at the door of death with my foot already over the line . . . and it appeared I could not chase away the tap of death on my shoulder.

Anyone really watching . . . who knew my circumstances in even a small way . . . would know that all the grace meted out from the incredible Lord above had surely drained dry.

God reached out, grabbed me back from the abyss of despair, and began to make me well in places so deep I did not even know I was sick.

Jesus knew everything about me. He was there as I was shaped and formed in my mother's womb. He knew the injuries, the pitfalls, the devastations. And He saw the narrow journeys of my heart.

All my life, God alone saw what I did to cope and cover and survive. He watched all my sheer, pitiful human demises.

Finally, He backed me into a corner I could not get out of. Nor could I blame anyone else . . . or places or events . . . for how I got there.

This towering, scowling mountain of inferiority and shame had loomed over me all

my life. Had squeezed out my very air . . .
and had to be faced.

I began, finally, to dare it to exist no longer. I
screamed at its insidiousness. Spit at it.
Cursed its lie. This monster of shame had
finally sucked every ounce of dignity and
self-respect and clear conscience from me.

I faced this mountain of captivity until it
began to tremble, to shake at its very
foundation.

For years, I tried to ignore and cover the
shame in me . . . even as a little girl pulls her
skirt around her legs for dignity and
protection. I was exhausted from its grip,
weak from the immovable hold on my one,
simple life. Like the Count of Monte Cristo, I
had spent years . . . almost my entire life . . .
clawing through endless rock. Seeking to
grasp how I could have lost the simple
pleasures and freedoms that once were mine.

The lie. The deception. It kept saying I was
loathsome and undeserving of peace. It kept
me reaching outside myself for peace and

forced me to live behind a persona of what everyone wanted me to be.

Until two years ago, I never knew who I really was. In these pages I will speak the truth, to the best of my ability, so the darkness can never again have reign over me. Force it into the light. The mountain that for so long had terrorized me can be no more.

I longed to feel freedom rising in my throat. The sweet, liquid taste of being unfettered. Relief running out my ears and nose and eyes, and down my soul. To be lost in the commotion of courageous men and women who boldly face the truth . . . looking deep within themselves. I wanted to be washed and cleansed by the sanctity of finally coming home.

With Martin Luther King Jr., I share this impassioned cry: "Free at last! Free at last! Thank God Almighty, [I am] free at last!"

With caution, I would like to share with you how God clipped the veil of my heart. How

He lovingly, carefully, began to show me all
the ways my heart had deceived me.

It was as if the heavy curtain that shrouded
and distracted the truth had to be painfully
yanked away. Like pulling scabs off very sore
wounds.

Through this journey, *I discovered the mystery of
divine grace. Of God's vast love that stoops for
broken mortals.* I will never be the same.

When you go through deep waters, and great trouble, I will be with you. When you go through rivers of difficulty, you will not drown! . . . (Isaiah 43:2)

One

Two years ago, I boarded a plane with our four children (seven, eight, ten, and eleven years old) and flew to California. Very dear friends, Herb and Dona, knew our family was in severe crisis and put feet to their love. They provided for the children and me while I got help . . . and spent many hours with Will helping him deal with his own issues. Before our journey was over, they put thousands of dollars and almost as many hours into our lives.

I could no longer lie to myself or the world. In my mind, amid the crisis, it was Will Anderson's fault. My downfall was his doing. I blamed him.

At the end of my human resources, divorce was still not in my vocabulary, but separation was. Resentful, enraged, and terrified, I truly believed that if I got away from Will, I would return to vibrance and health.

After our wedding and through fifteen years of marriage, I developed some serious health problems for the first time in my life. I underwent fifteen major operations. Miscarriages. Abdominal pain and kidney infections. I can still remember the first morphine shot. I had never had one before, and it quickly numbed the pain and sedated the sadness and inadequacies of my life. The inferiority. The anger. The frustrations.

I became very tired. Emotionally empty. All the years of trying to be so nice that no one could reject me. All the smiles. The pleasing and accommodating. Pain pills began to comfort me. I loved the sense of well-being I suddenly had.

It has always been paramount to me to appear healthy, happy, and whole . . . even perfect. To be strong. Impenetrable. Fearless. Daring. Weakness must NOT exist. I must be worthy of the *Good Housekeeping* seal of approval.

My children must look darling. We needed to appear prosperous as a family. Our marriage almost enviable.

Arriving in Fresno with the children was paralyzing. I knew no one. Fresno had been chosen because of a Christian counseling center, Link Care. We arrived on Memorial Day weekend, and everyone at Link Care was gone.

I had a serious kidney infection when I arrived. My doctor in Chicago had me on morphine pills, but I came with only a few, not knowing that if I stopped that medication abruptly, it could send my body into shock . . . and comas. Within twenty-four hours, my body did exactly that.

The infection made me very, very sick, and sudden withdrawal from pain pills left me in

agony and terror! I ended up in two very
serious comas, awakening in two Intensive
Care Units with IVs, tubes, and monitors. It
was terrifying, to say nothing of the physical
torture from withdrawal and the infection.

I was alone. The children were scared. *And
finally, God had my full attention.*

I was sick. Sick at the very core of my being.
I had lived with a heart turned in all
directions. Infected with fear and self. I lived
with an emptiness of not knowing who I was.

I was so sick, and Jesus came. He began to
turn my heart toward light. He peeled away
massive layers of niceness and good deeds
until the polluted, self-absorbed core was
exposed.

Yet He looked at me as if the sickness did not
even show.

Jan, my twin, flew in to take care of the
children, and I checked myself into a secular
drug treatment program. The most terrifying,
desperate journey of my life began. If Jan

had not been here with the children, I could *never* have done it. Because the struggle became so gut-wrenching, I needed to know the children felt intimate and safe, for all my strength was focused on survival . . . then healing.

I will let Jan begin the story:

All my life, I had watched Ann soar and achieve. For years, she seemed more a part of me than I was. Her achievements proudly announced in a phone call while at college or while teaching in a distant city seemed to bring me tranquillity. Almost like a drug to my brain. We and God would somehow make life work . . . succeed . . . past our dark childhoods of such great insignificance.

We were now fifty years old. Mothers, wives. A lot of life had begun to crumble for both of us. By following my husband, Tom, to a new job, I had just made a huge move in my life to a new city after twenty-two stable years of being a marriage and family therapist. I was hanging limply on to life myself.

I was awakened by the ringing of the telephone. A man on the other end speaking urgently. "Get your belongings in a bag NOW. Are you hearing me? I will give you the details while you pack."

(This was Herb Fisher, who, along with his wife, Dona, ended up putting more money and more stress than they had ever dreamed of into helping Ann and Will in their crisis.)

My eyes still closed, I put my feet over the side of the bed. Opening my eyes slightly, I stumbled to my closet, dragging the phone behind me. I grabbed for my bag and began, in a stupor, to pull clothes off hangers and shelves.

I really came to consciousness when this man said I was to be on a plane in an hour. How outrageous, I thought, until I was told that Ann and the boys were in California. Ann in a coma, hospitalized . . . and they needed me to take care of the boys.

Jarred back to reality by this man's voice, I

heard, "Your ticket is at the airport. Are you ready yet?"

Ready? I was still waking up!

I left that morning without saying good-bye to my child or husband, only calling them briefly from the airport. Stunned. I had helped people through things like this for years, but I was numb. In shock. I had better pull myself together quickly for my great leader!

It took me a day to get cross-country, and I was taken to the little motel where the children were being cared for. Taylor and Brock were still waiting up for me. The nurse at the ICU told me Ann was in critical condition, still unconscious.

The first emotion in trauma is DENIAL. At this point, I was shell-shocked and could accomplish no more than to crawl into bed and fall asleep.

I awoke early the next morning surrounded by Ann's four, beautiful, sleeping children. I grabbed frantically for my glasses and called the ICU. Ann's doctor said she was conscious, still in a guarded state, but I could come pick her up! Pick her up?! What did he mean? Now, you need to understand Ann pushed herself from the womb ten minutes before I did. She was one-and-a-half pounds heavier than I was. You may not consider that significant. I DO! From the womb, she was gathering strength to play out her place in our family. I grew up depending on her. From my earliest memories (three to four years old), she was designated by God to be the LEADER, and I was to be her FOLLOWER. No one had ever spoken it, but my bones and fiber knew this unequivocally.

She was smarter, and God had called me to one great mission: FOLLOW ANN! She knew God's ways. I had a lot of thoughts, but I do not think I talked for the first five years of life. Ann, at four years of age, was our spokesman. She knew. I did not know how. I just knew she did. And she was powerfully persuasive.

The doctor said we should come and pick Ann up. This was an outrageous idea to me, but I gathered every impressive piece of my knowledge and experience as a therapist. I insisted the doctor send her with her medication until I could figure out my next step. No one detoxes in twenty-four hours!

God and His angels were with that doctor. He listened. The children and I drove to the hospital. I wanted to go back to being four years old when she was in control.

The next four weeks were the journey of a blind man with a white cane tapping one way and then another for direction and truth. I was led from darkness to light again and again.

I moved us to a slightly better motel and gave Ann a couple of pills to keep her alive until my empty brain and paralyzed heart could figure out what to do. I was as lost as her twelve-year-old son, Taylor. She lay down and did not move for twelve more hours. I could not arouse her. Denial is an awesome thing, and most people underestimate its survival power. I took her pulse every few minutes and did what my father always did in times of crisis: PRAY. PRAY. PRAY.

"God, keep Ann alive. Why did that crazy hospital release her? Jesus, save us!" I screamed silently. "Save us!" She was so frail. After another ten hours of coma, I knew I'd better figure something out!

We carried her frail, unconscious body to the car, loaded up, and I drove into Fresno. I found a large hospital and drove to the emergency entrance.

We found the perfect detox treatment center for Ann. I moved four little boys and myself five times in four weeks. During those days, I felt as if both Ann and I were merely crawling like infants in circles. But at a backward glance, looking over my shoulder two years down the road, I can see the breathtaking, beautiful kaleidoscope of events only God could have put in place on our game board of life.

The pain . . . rage . . . humor . . . growth and camaraderie of mutual goals were all a part of the journey. I can see God really does have the whole world in His hands!

As for Taylor, Brock, Colson, and Brandt, I could not have had a greater team to go to war with the forces of evil. They were magnificent . . . optimistic . . . fun . . . obedient teammates. I fell hopelessly in love with each of them. We did everything from having therapy sessions to pooling our brainpower as to how we could rent videos without proof of residency. Every day we went to visit Ann with ice cream, magazines, and candy. These were the greatest days I have ever experienced with my LEADER! Her fear of these "mean, obnoxious, confronting roommates and other patients" would actually bring a deep throat release of laughter from me. I told her to give it back to them. "What can they do to you, Ann?"

Honestly, I made it through those four weeks with no sense of my own strength or even well-developed skills as a therapist. It

Ann Kiemel Anderson

had to have been God's strength. And in
many moments, God and the wonderful
couple helping Ann probably questioned
who they had called in for this assignment.

Ann has made it down the road now two
years without pills and fought with as much
determination as when she attacked any
marathon she ever ran. Her willingness to
tell her pure, human story makes her a
leader for all. She's blazed the trail for each
of us — if we will be courageous enough to
face our truest, darkest selves. And God did
know . . . I am still the follower by a long
shot . . . more than ten minutes!

Janet Kiemel Ream
Overland Park, Kansas

Even though the fig trees have no
blossoms,
And there are no grapes on the vine;
Even though the olive crop fails,
And the fields lie empty and barren;
Even though the flocks die in the fields,
And the cattle barns are empty;
Yet I will rejoice in the LORD!
I will be joyful in the God of my
salvation.
The Sovereign LORD is my strength! . . .
(Habakkuk 3:17–19)

Two

With hidden terror, I hugged and kissed my children's warm, soft faces . . . and Jan's . . . and walked into Cedar Vista, a psychiatric hospital, which had a wing specifically dealing with chemical dependency.

No one behind those locked doors cared about my past successes. The sad and broken . . . all of us . . . were on level ground. We had all been to the doors of hell and back, using chemicals to numb the wounds rather than courage to look deep within.

Like all the others, I was clueless about how bad off I was, even after two near-fatal comas. I minimized my pill use. I blamed it all on Will. The others credited sad luck in life or others' mistreatment of them. We were a sorry lot.

I simply wanted to detox and get on with my life. After all, I had not spent the majority of my life on pills! This did not seem too complicated. Scary, but reasonable.

There were two group sessions every day, each with a different therapist. A petite blonde, also a pill addict, was in the program with me. At my very first session, she confronted me in group: "Ann, you are the most pathetic person I have ever seen. You are sickening. Just looking at you is my impetus never to use again. You think you are so good. Well, you are a sorry excuse for humanity!"

Tears stung my eyes. I was shamed beyond imagination. I felt exposed. Naked. Terror

began to rise in my throat. I could taste it.
The physical trauma from withdrawal of the
morphine was agonizing, but being screamed
at and ridiculed was almost unimaginable.
She had been so syrupy nice right before the
session.

I had spent my entire life protecting myself
from rejection. The sting and torment I felt as
a small girl in Hawaii, different in color from
all the beautiful islanders, had led me to vow,
as a child, never to allow anyone to reject me
again. I would be too nice and too sweet and
too smart.

Now, an adult . . . a wife and mother . . . and
what I had so feared had come upon me!

Detoxing was a nightmare for me. My kidney
infection was full-blown, and though they
gave me antibiotics, I had nothing to ease the
terrible sickness from the infection.

I was so thin, too thin, and behind the doors
at Cedar Vista, I kept losing weight. There
was probably not one endorphin in my
body.

Almost without exception, everyone smoked.
A lot. I began to smell it in the walls. In the
carpets. In hair. In the dining room and the
food. I grew attached, quickly, to all those
around me. I loved hanging out with them,
but the cigarette smoke took what little
appetite I had away.

They gave me lots of glasses of vitamin
supplement drinks. The commercials on
television lie. They tasted awful!

Alcoholics, cocaine and heroin addicts! Pain
pill junkies. All kinds, and many came and
went while I was there. Most of them were
agnostic, and truly, for most, every other
word was an expletive. It was a different
environment from any I had ever been in.
The one thing we all had in common was the
devastation and calamity that using alcohol
and drugs had brought us. These were the
most courageous people I had ever been
around! Courageous because they had
enough internal strength to voice all their
failures. To hide nothing. To face all the
character defects.

I have often dropped names of important people. If you understand that I am connected to high-profile people then you will honor me. You will attach significance to my value. But Jesus says, "The first will be last, and to be a leader you must first be a servant." I confess this self-absorbed pretense, and today am depending on God's grace to help me walk simply and humbly. After all, no one cares about who I know. No one . . . but me.

Performance, for most of life, had been my drug of choice. Be smart. Be trim. Run races, and win. Give glowing speeches. Make A's. Do not just run 10Ks. Take on 26.2-mile marathons.

I am sad that I needed — demanded — to share the praise with God. Telling the world about the gymnasium God inspired me to build in the Boston ghetto. Yet, making sure everyone knew my hard-earned money paid for it.

Then there were the marathons. I spoke and wrote of that magnificent dream . . . running and singing little songs to other runners about Jesus. Yet, I also made sure everyone knew it was my feet that hit the pavement. My courage that persevered.

Singing little songs to neighbors and on planes I traveled was a sincere gesture from my heart. However, as Christians started applauding me for it, I suddenly felt I had to do it more. If that was what the world admired, I had better make it more of my focus.

Everything I did became motivated by two forces. One, my sincere love for others and wanting to allow God to use me in touching them with love. And two, my hunger to be loved and praised. In reality, the forces conflicted with each other, and my integrity began disintegrating in the most subtle ways. Unnoticed by others for a long while, and obviously deluding my convictions in a way I could not see.

In Cedar Vista, I could not understand this. I simply was blind! I longed to perform because that was my way, in all the years past, to succeed. To have favor. But I could not perform in this environment. It was a foreign arena to me, and regardless, they were trained in that unit to see all the behaviors typical to addicts.

They wanted me to say I was an addict. I resisted this. Becoming dependent on pills and being an addict were two different things to me.

And when I tried to paint a sad picture of the things Will had done to me . . . and the misfortunes of my life . . . they set me straight. Will may have issues, but he was not to blame for my ending up there.

Everyone was to journal each day, turning our notebooks in for the therapists to read before the sessions. I am a writer. Sixteen books to my credit. Yet, not once could I journal correctly.

The others' notebooks would be returned with comments of "good" or "great job!" My journal was handed back with a sense of exasperation. Written in the margins were comments like "Ann, you are in denial!" or "You do not get it, do you!"

I *was* in denial. I prided myself on the fact
that my pill use was only because of broken
health. I had never, unlike others, illegally
written my own prescriptions (I was never
that creative!). I had not been to jail or been
waiting for a court date like many of the
others. Nor was I homeless.

For the first nine days, I did not sleep. Not at
all. To articulate the physical misery would
be impossible. Even today, two years down
the road, it hurts to reminisce. I felt like Job.
Destitute. Racked by unbelievable pain,
emotional and physical. My skin crawling.
The shakes. My insides gnawing and raw.
And oh! the terror of night!

Night moved into my soul like a liquid
despair, ready to devour me. Especially being
away from my children.

As midnight approached, everyone else
would be sleeping. I felt myself being
irresistibly drawn into a journey of
paralyzing panic. I paced the halls. Took
several hot baths nightly. Fought the dragons
in my mind by clinging to the thread around

my heart that was attached to God's strong arm of mercy.

Night after night after night. Alone. I felt I was in a wheelbarrow, balanced on a tightrope that stretched for miles over a raging, rushing ocean below. There was no way I was going to make it if God did not intervene and provide a miracle. The dark currents below were waiting to swallow me in death.

Again, Jan being with the children was the one stabilizing force in the midst of all this pain.

For most of my twenty-five days in Cedar Vista, I had a roommate that was in worse shape than I. And except for the fact that she at least made me, in comparison, look a little sane, she was the most unpleasant, miserable, and angry person I had ever met.

Unlike me, she slept almost ALL the time. Day and night. During the long nights, I would tiptoe in and lie in my bed, hoping . . . praying . . . to fall asleep. When it did not work, I would get up and tiptoe out.

However, my roommate would lift her head and yell at me to be quiet. To shut up. If she did awake while I was silently lying there, she would jump up and start fumbling for her cigarettes. If she could not find them, she would accuse me of taking them. Me, the only non-smoker

I spent many night hours lying in my bed, praying for her. How much it meant to know I had Jesus . . . and beautiful memories of my father's unswerving faith and my mother's love. It seemed she could not find her way out of any of it.

I longed for sleep. For relief. For even an hour when my eyes would close, and my body, racked with pain, could be forgotten. I longed for it. Prayed for it. Begged God to bless me with it. But sleep eluded me . . . like a rainbow just beyond my grasp . . . and my terror and misery crescendoed.

Whoever stubbornly refuses to accept criticism
Will suddenly be broken beyond repair.
(Proverbs 29:1)

Three

Anyone who knew me at all would have known that the way to start really penetrating the thick barricade of layers around my heart was simply to attack my motherhood.

Nothing on earth, aside from having Christ, compared to the love and adoration I felt for my four children. I love them with every fiber of my being, and being separated from them hurt the most.

One afternoon, in our group session, the fiery, volatile woman in our group continued her screaming at me: "Ann, you aren't any better than the rest of us. Do not tell me you have been a good mother. You have [expletive] all over your kids, and I feel so sorry for them."

I let out a groan that erupted from the deepest core of me. A groan that rose in my throat, filled every room, and left me shaking and crying.

The children had gone on dozens of trips with me to the doctors. They had spent hours in hospital emergency rooms, waiting with Will while the doctors cared for me.

Through all my physical ailments, I had never understood that pain and buried rage and compromise had contributed on a huge scale to the breaking down of my body. That when, in wanting to be a passive, submissive wife, I swallowed all that was wrong with Will and me, and stuffed and stuffed. I chose misery at times, rather than taking a stand on what was not right. Also so much pain medicine further attacked my immune system.

I had spent hours . . . and years reading to my children. Snuggling with them. Empathizing with their bruises and bumps. Each night I, even to this day, lie next to each child in the dark, at bedtime, and let them tell me their deepest thoughts. Bedtime and darkness somehow give children a way of expressing their deepest thoughts.

I baked dozens and dozens of cookies and muffins . . . and little homemade cakes at bedtime.

But I was not what I should have been. I was not honest enough or integrated enough to face my hidden pain and many issues. I was a kid myself. I loved bike rides and ice cream and sunshine and snacks and kisses, and hot chocolate with the boys when it was cold and blustery out.

The children needed more structure and responsibility . . . and a mother who knew peace. A mother who was awake.

I was scared and unsure and fearful and angry. But I did not see it. I still could not.

The third day in Cedar Vista, the physician-in-charge (a recovering addict himself), Dr. Rich Guzetta, sat down with me. Within minutes, he looked at me and said, "Ann, you are not getting this. The therapists say you are a problem. You are in total denial. From here you must go to a full year of in-house treatment in some other facility!"

I gaped at him, stunned. "A year of in-house treatment? You have got to be kidding! That is INSANE. I am here with my four, young children . . ."

"Well, if you are not willing to do this, I will release you now!"

More than stunned. Angry. Enraged. "Go ahead! Dismiss me. I will not go anywhere for a year."

Two weeks, maybe. But a YEAR?! No one had remotely hinted at such a requirement. He might think I was very sick . . . but I was just now beginning to adjust to the idea that I might be an addict!

The doctor got up and marched out, leaving me with my heart thumping in my throat. I stumbled out, looking for a phone.

"Jan, come and get me. Now! No, I have not detoxed completely, but the doctor is sending me home . . ."

Jan was thrown into her own tailspin. *Ann's being dismissed? How can that be?* She called Link Care and got a therapist on the line.

"Do something . . . I don't care what you have to do. Ann cannot come home before she at least detoxes."

The doctor was called. He agreed to work with me no matter what. I, with a bruised heart, unpacked my things and tried to nurse my wounds.

I do not understand all the logistics of what happened that day. Today, I know Dr.

Guzetta was fighting for me. He was trying to get my attention.

From that day on, the tide began to turn. Very slowly. A sliver of light . . . of truth . . . began to dawn.

Eight days later, I sat across from Dr. Guzetta in a small room. Pale. Too thin. No makeup. Hair pulled back in a ponytail. Misery etched across my face. My body tight . . . emotionally and physically exhausted.

Nine days without sleep. Still experiencing terrible sweats and raw insides. *But I had endured enough to taste freedom* . . . just a little . . . and it tasted more wonderful than anything I had ever known. With tears in my eyes, I spoke:

"Dr. Guzetta, I have decided there is nothing I will not do to be set free from my addictions. NOTHING. If you tell me I have to go somewhere for a year, I will. God will work out my marriage and caring for the children."

He spoke to me in almost a whisper. As if too much noise or abruptness might alter the healing course I was on. "This is a miracle. An absolute miracle. I can never tell who is going to make it in this program."

The issue of spending a year in another treatment center, long term, was never mentioned again. After twenty-five days, I was released . . . and that was two years ago.

The secret was in surrender. Letting go. Letting God. AA has a little saying: "Let go. Let God. He can."

All the years I took pills, I prayed God would zap me. Just deliver me in an instant. A split second. Delivered. Physically healed. Emotionally whole. Free.

I had heard testimonials on Christian television. God knew, however, that only in facing myself . . . only in unrelenting honesty could I be set free. And God knew that I was a tough case. One of those "sicker than most."

I was blind. The powers of darkness had dimmed my eyes. It took many days without sleep to break me down. To pull the blinders from my eyes.

No sleep. Being so often targeted in the therapy sessions (I think I got blasted every day!). And total failure in knowing how to perform. God knew this was exactly what it would take to crack my diseased heart and that Cedar Vista was the place this could be achieved.

I have chosen you and will not throw you away. Don't be afraid, for I am with you. Do not be dismayed, for I am your God. I will strengthen you. I will help you. I will uphold you with my victorious right hand. (Isaiah 41:9-10)

Four

Jan would bring the children to Cedar
Vista to visit me. I lived for the moments
to simply spot them coming through the
door. They always wore fresh, glowing
smiles.

Sometimes, Jan would come by herself.
She was fabulous with the boys. Had a
baby-sitter play ball with them. Took
them to ride go-carts and to do other
very fun activities.

Always, when she came, I was so sick.

So unbelievably miserable. Clinging to her, I would tell her about the last group session. About all the confrontations. That I simply felt singled out.

Jan said, "Ann, what are you afraid of? So terrified about?"

"I don't know. The therapist said I displayed histrionic behavior. What does that mean?"

Jan would tell me there was nothing anyone could say that would finish me off. That I might listen and choose only what made sense to address in myself. However, my terror remained. Every session, I felt everyone was undressing me. Leaving me naked and bare and exposed.

I had been very careful to protect myself all through life. Even as a small child, I did not voice anything that might put me in a bad light. I would scold Jan if she even hinted at a less than top grade in school.

"Jan, do not tell anyone you got a C! They will think you are not smart."

She would look at me, dismayed. Why would anyone think that?

One of the first things I told Dr. Guzzetta upon arrival was that I had authored many books. Hoping to say anything that would make me acceptable and special. Impressing others was a well-honed trade with me. Dr. Guzzetta, rather than being impressed, actually thought I was delusional. Fortunately, one of the nurses found a book I had written, and my future in an institution was spared.

The very thing Kris and Georgette, the therapists, wanted from me was the exact thing I had guarded against all my life. They wanted me to look, with unadorned honesty, deep within myself. To address core issues from my family of origin. What were the secrets in my life? Any? What had created the buried rage and resentment? . . . because addictions to drugs and alcohol are symptomatic of much bigger problems. That triggered the therapists' reactions. "Why is anger a sin?" they asked. It was simply an emotion, created by God. Only how we dealt with it determined right from wrong.

One day a therapist wrote in my journal, "Quit smiling! Deal with your resentments!"

Again, I was stunned. I did not know I lived with a smile on my face. If so, why was that so bad?

Cedar Vista has built its entire chemical dependency unit around Alcoholics Anonymous. I vaguely remembered hearing the term "AA", but was clueless.

I do recall a man who invited my father to an AA meeting, just as his friend. It was one of the most thrilling experiences my father ever spoke about. The honesty, the confessions. Speaking on a first-name-only basis. Daddy was captivated, and closing with the others in the Lord's Prayer thrilled him too. I never, today, stand in one of those circles without it moving me as well.

Twelve years ago, I had been cared for by RAPHA, a Christian psychiatric facility. I

felt it was high-class, with outstanding staff.
They were very kind to me, but at that point,
I do not remember addiction being the top
priority. I had been taking pills for a couple
of years but basically felt the focus was on
my relationship with Will. Regardless, my
heart was cloaked with denial, and I simply
had not come close to bottoming out. It was
my first experience in trying to figure out my
problems. Within six weeks of returning
home from RAPHA, I was spiraling down to
rock bottom again. Nothing had really
changed in me or in my relationship with
Will.

During the long night hours in Cedar Vista,
pacing the halls, I would stand and read the
twelve steps, individually framed and
hanging along the walls. I was spellbound by
these steps because God was the overriding
theme. In such a secular environment, I was
hungry for more of God. For someone simply
to pray with me.

During days and nights, I would mark small,
invisible increments on my arm. Always, I
challenged myself to keep going for thirty-

minute segments. My kidney infection, my skin crawling, the sweats, and the stark aloneness were so painful that my courage and willpower could only face small amounts of time.

> Learning to lean
> Learning to lean
> I'm learning to lean on Jesus.
> Finding more power
> than I've ever seen . . .
> I'm learning to lean on Jesus.

This was my song every day. We were shown videos on addiction almost every day. Pounded into our thinking was the reality that only a tiny percentage ever make it. Most alcoholics and addicts relapse again and again. Almost without exception, everyone who walked through the doors of Cedar Vista had been in and out of detox units for years. I was in a minority.

The fact that few really make it was the most terrifying of all. I had to make it. There were no other options. I could *never* go down this road again. NEVER. NEVER. If it meant every day for a year, I would have to stand on

my head in some corner. I did not care what
it took. Tell me and I would do it.

With an addict mind, you cannot turn a
corner unless everything in your thinking has
been stripped. If there is one nickel left . . .
one detour . . . it still has power over you.
With me, I had nothing left.

The nurses and therapists would bring home
the point over and over:

"There are fifteen of you here. Only two . . .
maybe three if you're lucky . . . of you are
going to go out there and stay clean. And the
first year is the very hardest. If you can get
through the first twelve months, the chances
are much greater for ongoing recovery."

A year! I could taste it, yet behind the doors
of Cedar Vista, it still seemed way beyond my
grasp. Impossible.

Jesus, please help me to be one of the two. Please . . .

When I walked into Cedar Vista, I fully
believed that once the pills were out of my

system, I could proceed to live a productive, pill-free life. But, they were telling us it was not that simple.

The head nurse cautioned us. He said, "You will not remember the misery of detox. Our natural bent is to forget the pain. You need better tools to help you stay away from the substances."

Two years down the road, I assure you my memory does not allow me to forget the awful torture of those twenty-five days. God understood, I think, that with me I needed to remember the hellish darkness that must not be repeated.

One video was on the "three-headed dragon." That drinking or using is only one piece of this complex problem. It is only the symptom of much deeper holes that we are trying to fill. Unless we grow up emotionally and learn to break down the denial (mind-intellect), we will never be able to abstain from mind-altering substances. Will never learn the skills of approaching life's issues with health. Of not numbing the pain or despair.

Today, this is understandable . . . reasonable.
Two years ago, I was groping in total
darkness. I was a newborn, screaming . . .
scared.

I was a little girl in an adult body. On the
outside, I was married . . . a mother . . . with
God's love and a career. But behind the
persona, I had not been able to grow beyond
the pain of my childhood.

The empty, gaping wounds of my childhood
had kept me enslaved. Stunted. Protective.
The gaping insignificance I lived with as a
little girl followed me everywhere. The
smiling and performing and pills simply
numbed the hurt, allowing the pain to fester.

I began to look back . . . to relive my
childhood. Hoping to find some clues about
what had brought me to such a catastrophic
place. It became very clear to me that
performance and praise had been all-out
addictions since childhood. Since I, at four,
made a little girl color with me and appointed
Jan as the judge. Jan quickly realized she
was in a no-win situation and whispered to

me that mine was the prettiest but she would say the other girl's name to make her feel good.

Before I could understand my pill taking (not when I was truly sick, but when it was more and more for emotional comfort), I had to understand it was simply the final phase in my coping escapes. *Codependency was my first book.*

Come to Me, all of you who are weary and carry heavy burdens, and I will give you rest. Take My yoke upon you. Let Me teach you, because I am humble and gentle, and you will find rest for your souls. (Matthew 11:28-29)

Five

Remembering Childhood . . . Hawaii

It was Sunday, or Tuesday. It could have
been any day. We would pile into the car
for a drive or to go hear my father
preach somewhere.

"Everybody happy? Say, 'Amen'!"

This was not some silly routine of mine.
It was paramount to my sense of security
and well-being.

I said, "Amen." Jan did. My mother would say it with a tiny curve to her mouth, which meant "Do we have to do this again?" That left my father.

"Oh, honey, don't make me say that . . ."

"Daddy, aren't you happy? Well, why not? Oh, please, Daddy, just say 'Amen.'"

My father would display a silent heave, and quietly say, "Amen."

Yahoo! I was happy. I was suddenly given my ticket to joy. My well-being was completely enmeshed with the temperament of those around me. The "amen" ritual took place *every* time we got in the car.

Codependency came as naturally as breathing to me. There was such a sense of sadness with my daddy, and it became my mission to make him happy . . . so I could be happy.

My father was a holy, gentle man whose highs and lows came from my brother's behavior and the church's response to his preaching.

My mother never appeared unhappy, even in the worst of times, and she became my hiding place.

Fred, almost six years older than Jan and me, was volatile and angry. He appeared to hate all of us and life in general. Today, I think my father was incapable of capturing Fred's heart and put too narrow a rein on him.

Jan, my identical twin who was ten minutes younger, was more or less what I was. She appeared less influenced by the moods in our house, so she followed me, and we became comrades in terror and fear. I was her protector.

We moved to Hawaii when I was eight so my father could pastor a church there. I still remember my first day of school. Jan and I, donned in beautiful dresses sewed by my mother, walked into an all-Oriental elementary school.

Pigtails and blue eyes and pale skin.
Everyone else was so dark. Brown skin,
flashing eyes, and straight hair that
glimmered in the sunlight. Glistening. And
everyone's teeth were so white. Was it their
dark lips and skin that did that to their teeth?

I stood in one spot, staring. Everyone was
beautiful. Everyone's skin was flawless. The
girls were so pretty. The oriental twins. They
were knockouts, yet people began to
compare us to them.

"No comparison!" I wanted to scream. "There
is no comparison! They are beautiful . . .
gorgeous . . . and we are not!"

To this day, I do not recall their faces being
special. It was simply their olive skin and
beautiful clothes . . . different ones every day.

Before third grade in Hawaii, there are
vague, dim images of some school recesses . . .
playground encounters in Portland, Oregon,
when I longed to be with those kids over
there. They seemed popular and special. But
when they asked me to join them, I quickly

realized they were not that fun. I longed to return to the kids scattered here and there where no pressure to act giddy and snobbish was demanded.

I felt confused. Somehow wherever I was at a given time turned out not to feel as fun as being somewhere else.

I feared I would say or do something that was not perfectly right or good. My insides were swarming with emotions. Always conflicting, always feeling less than. Always admiring others' beauty and shaming my own.

If a shepherd has one hundred sheep, and one wanders away and is lost, what will he do? Won't he leave the ninety-nine others and go out into the hills to search for the lost one?
(Matthew 18:12)

Six

There was love and surprise and God and sit-down dinners and breakfasts at our house. But, also, there was hostility that shook the veiled, tender corners of my heart.

The focus was Fred, my brother. He thought and felt and viewed everything differently from the rest of us. In my house, though my father was a holy man . . . honorable . . . the hostility tightened our hearts if anyone disagreed with Daddy's view of God or the way he defined our words and attitudes.

With Daddy, there were morning prayers prayed only by him. They had to be long enough and beseeched with passion for the eternal Lord of the universe to hear or beckon our way. Whether we were late to school or breakfast was not finished or our teeth yet unbrushed, it was time for prayer. For kneeling. For ignoring the clock. The time to listen to my father plead the blood of Jesus . . . to beg that every atom of sin and self be forgiven. I always prayed that Daddy would, one time, pray briefly.

How I longed to pray just one time. Something simple from my child's heart that in many ways was still fresh from God. *In a noise-shattered world, I longed for my heart to pierce the clamoring darkness.*

And though I adored my father, I was set aside, for God needed to hear from him. Or, he needed to assure himself that the ritual was carried out.

There was a rigidity about my father's thoughts
and feelings that dragged me to an abyss of
powerlessness and anger. I never dared allow
the anger to seep through. It simply continued
to mount, unnoticed, to all but our God.

I confess Jan and I tried to distract my father
from morning worship, but it never worked.
We were talking to God. Do you
understand? We were . . . or rather Harold
Kiemel was having an intimate talk with God
about all his tribulations and struggles, and
none of us could proceed to the next thing on
our agendas until his praying was done.

It was very frustrating, but I look back and
feel great respect for my father's unfaltering
allegiance to God. He taught me Jesus pays.
Gilorious and absolute.

This praying was done on our knees. No
sitting down before a holy God. My knees
would get red. I squirmed. I felt resentment
that none of us could do the Bible reading or
prayer. It was Daddy's job, he felt, to pray
the demons away. I do not think any of us

knew exactly what these demons were. That was secret information between Daddy and God.

Maybe Fred could not tolerate the rigid, tightly strung band that called our lives into functional existence. I do not know. I am sure that Fred, different from Jan and me, refused the imprisonment that lifestyle offered him.

It made Fred overtly angry and enraged all the time. A frown lived between his brows. A tone of voice that sent me to hide under pillows or in my bedroom closet.

I remember fire, loud and close to lethal, whenever my parents found a pack of cigarettes or caught Fred smoking. In my mind, smoking and murder were side by side, and both demanded long prison terms, if not death.

One day, I got this notion that Fred hid his cigarettes in the toe of his shoes. Pushed down to the points, he would then stuff his socks in behind them.

I knew. No one hinted it to me. No one challenged me to check it out. But I KNEW. With heart pounding like some electric drum, I tiptoed in . . . pulled out the socks . . . and there were two packs of cigarettes. Filthy things right from the devil's private workshop. I grabbed them. Replaced the socks. Straightened the shoes, and I was out of there.

As you might have expected, Fred found them. Well, he found the shoes without the cigarettes. Rage . . . that could probably cause an extinct volcano to erupt . . . came after me. This rage that turned his eyes into flames and formed perspiration on his brow.

He came storming toward me. His face was nearly touching mine, and I was not sure what he might do to me. So I stood still . . . deathly so . . . and almost without breath.

"Did you take my cigarettes?" he screamed. "Yes," I replied, staring at him.

Would he murder me? Or cripple me? I was not sure. The only thing I knew was I had

told the truth . . . though not where I had
hidden the cigarettes.

In a few seconds that felt for certain like
hours, he glared at me and walked away.

I never told my parents, for I feared my
father would start into his ten-day fast of not
eating or drinking . . . to pray . . . and die.

Seven

My mother was my ideal. She was beautiful and easygoing and brilliant. She could sew anything. Cook meals we loved. Play jazz and old hymns at bedtime. She gave us room to be unhappy. To scream and be frustrated. And she always forgave us without any fuss.

My world felt so conflicting. Music and art and yummy food and daily prayers and much love and intimacy from my father and mother. Yet . . .

the ongoing hostility and rage and frustration
between my father and my brother. It
ricocheted onto us.

I was too young to understand the bigger
picture, and today, everything is frozen into
memory banks, sealed forever when I was a
child.

Several abiding truths of my early life are
embedded in my very fiber.

First, I did feel and know my parents loved
God and me. They never wavered.

Second, my brother communicated, without
ever using words, but by his anger and
sullenness, that I must be less than nothing.
That I was worthy of no one, and that just
seeing me probably filled him with disgust.
That is how I *perceived* his thoughts of me.

Today, Fred and I are close. He says he never
felt all those things about me. That the
messages I visually or audibly received were
nothing more than the shrapnel sprayed on

me from his and Daddy's screaming and
fighting.

The noise came from the basement. From
riding in the car. From the sound of the belt.
From Fred cursing. The noise never led to
some good conclusions. It simply magnified
the pain and rage.

Fred would crawl up on the roof and smoke
so my parents could not see him. My mother
was horrified because the neighbors could
see him, and that was worse.

He would stay out until all hours of the night,
leaving my father to pace and pray. I never
went to sleep at night without listening to my
father beseech God, mostly for Fred. Jan and
I were included briefly, but of course, we
were not one step from hell like Fred. Who
would die first? Fred or my dad? That was
most of what I thought about. Why would
Fred not invite Jesus into his heart? Why?
Why was he never happy? It was a global
issue in my mind.

Those who search for me will surely find me.
(Proverbs 8:17)

Eight

My hair was combed into two ponytails . . . with ribbons . . . and I wore a pretty dress my mother had made. She would go downtown. Study children's designer clothes . . . and come home to copy them for us.

My patent leather shoes were buckled, and I sat next to Jan. She was my identical twin, and the one with whom I held back no secrets. My father, so sincere and sweet, but never spectacular in his preaching, had concluded his Sunday message. Would we all please turn to a hymn for closing?

There was always a purpose for this hymn. The songs were always pleading for us to come to Jesus. They had sad melodies. People were challenged in a desperate-love manner to come forward and pray.

"Let the Lord Jesus cleanse you. Come and be free. Come to Jesus today!"

Our church always had an altar for those who came. A place where each could kneel and cry out to Jesus.

The piano, played by my mother, sounded the chords, and everyone began singing.

This part of the service was what I most feared and dreaded. Though only eight, then nine, and then ten, I knew Jesus. I had walked the long aisle in public confession.

But my brother had not. He had failed to make his repentance of sin before all. He needed to because he and my daddy had terrible, loud run-ins. I often tucked my legs under my dress and waited in terror for the murder to take place. It was noise I could not understand. There were yelling and meanness and crying and pushing.

I begged God to help Fred down the aisle. I wanted it so, yet it loomed a bigger miracle than blind men seeing. It always seemed beyond our grasp.

The last verse was sung, and Daddy said we must sing it one more time. We must . . . for someone was yearning to come to Jesus. I knew the only someone my father was trying to coerce down the aisle was Fred.

If Fred would go, our lives would be happy. My father would quit praying and crying and come to the dinner table. On the last few words of the last verse of the altar call, I would quickly move out and down the aisle, and kneel at the altar.

I knew Jesus. I could not think of any new sins, yet I went, a lonely, earnest child in pigtails. Maybe my father would not be so sad if at least one of his children was there. *I was the peace offering.*

Week after week, I went forward. Song after song after stirring message on God's love but hell to pay without Jesus. My brother always stood in his pew.

I continued to shoulder the burden of my daddy's unhappiness. And my mother, who would buy fabric that she said was a "steal" and show Jan and me pattern ideas . . . well, it was unthinkable for me to say I did not like the fabric or the pattern design.

We would rave. Give her a hug. Act enthusiastic. Inside, Jan and I were sad we had nothing faddish. Like the other kids. My mother's taste was impeccable, but I never felt "in." Be honest at the risk it might hurt her? NEVER!

Thus, the strength to be honest was washed away to some dark place in my heart where I could not even remember where it was or if it had ever existed.

Nine

Continuing Childhood

It was a surprise event. We had been invited to the Hemrys' for dessert. Invited out! I loved when someone in our church asked us over. There were no televisions or fancy toys at our house. Going visiting was . . . well . . . going visiting. But it was something special to fill the time.

I loved listening to adults talk. I loved just being around people. The smells in a house. The pictures on the walls.

Another family's flavor. Listening to chitchat.
It was creative.

"Mommy. PLEASE don't make us play with
the children. Jan and I want to listen to the
adults. Promise, Mommy!"

She would usually volunteer us.

"The twins would love to go play . . ." "Let the
twins do the dishes. They are great at that!"

For a reason I don't remember, my parents
decided Fred had to go to the Hemrys' too.
We were a family after all. It was time we
acted like one. It showed respect. Honor.

All hell broke loose. All the craziness and
yelling and rebelling and screaming.

Fred said he would NOT go. My father said
he would. My mother stood with my father.
One time shouldn't hurt him. After all, they
had a fine, teenage son.

"Fred, we almost never make you go.
Tonight, we are insisting!"

More screaming and hollering, but Harold Kiemel was immovable. I was sure every neighbor could hear. Sirens would sound any minute. The police would rush in. And probably the Buddhist temple across the street from our house would even start beating the gong.

Mother and Jan and I got in the backseat of the car, which was parked in front of the church. We, for a time, lived in the back of the church.

Fred was hollering. My dad, not particularly strong or big, was dragging Fred by the arms. They somehow got to the car, with my father ordering Fred to get in.

Fred yelled something awful, which, in simple terms, explained he would not. Not then. Not ever! Daddy gave Fred a shove. Fred grabbed my father. Before my grade school eyes, I watched them wrestle and fight. One will against the other.

Jan and I were crying, screaming, "They are going to kill each other!"

"No . . . No . . . ," my mother whispered.

"Yes, Fred is going to kill Daddy!"

At that point, I was crouched, with Jan, on the floor in the backseat. Hands over our heads. Crying harder.

I do not know how it all came to be . . . but Fred did go. We walked in quietly . . . our faces solemn. Our voices strained.

The Hemrys never knew. The ride home was mute, and a tired moroseness dangled in the air. All the excitement and fun had died long hours before we ever got there.

Fred asked my father to perform his marriage to a beautiful girl named Sandy in a Catholic church because Sandy was Catholic. However, we knew Fred's marrying a Catholic was another very dark sign. Catholics were a dangerous lot. Maybe communists. That's what I thought. I assure you that was an eleven year old's reasoning.

I still remember my father tucking a little
New Testament under Fred's arm at the
airport and hugging him good-bye as he left
on his honeymoon . . . and to true adulthood.
It was the first real act of love and compassion
I ever saw my brother and father have.

This hostility draped itself around my heart. I
grew up in confusion.

Anger scared me. It seemed unleashed in our
house when Fred was there. Fred's anger was
probably always directed at my father, but it
never felt that way. We were all absorbed in the
pain around Fred. Any problems or struggles I
had were so minuscule compared to this
darkness that I never felt them worthy of
attention.

And I somehow felt I was in the middle of the
struggle. Or the cause. The focus. I was
deserving of the noise . . . the screams. The
madness. And I felt that Fred was more
loathing of me than anyone.

Fred and I have made amends. It took me

twenty-five years to be courageous enough to ask him why he despised me. I am still stunned by his answer. "Ann, honey, I never felt anything bad about you! I was so absorbed in Daddy's and my conflict that I was oblivious to you. You got the shock waves. It was not about you!"

At the very genesis of my little-girl-coming-out process, a cavern took shape in me. Not the God-shaped vacuum, for I trusted Christ as a tiny girl. But the gorge where self-respect and individual worth should have been. I was filled with a shame . . . a repugnant sense of not even deserving citizenship.

Not once, as a child, do I remember Fred looking at me (except over the cigarettes) or speaking to me. I could not figure out what was so despicable and revolting to deserve this. I only believed his revulsion was there, and I must protect Jan.

And in the complicated journey by which a child sets about to live, I started along an arduous marathon of performance.

It did not seem important to know myself, but only to know what pleased others. If there was only shame in the very inner-weavings of myself, then I must do and go and be whatever would hide that . . . tightly conceal it . . . and bring me the love and kindness.

I had to have love. That beautiful, lovely, inanimate aura that made people smile at me and touch me and applaud my existence.

And I must never, at any cost, be lonely or pitied. Weak. Loneliness had walked with me from the beginning. Jan was there, my comrade and treasured friend, yet I, even with Jan, felt loneliness. She found friends easily. She was not afraid of herself. I felt she did not need me in the ways I needed her.

It is very difficult to write about Fred. He has two beautiful children whom I love very much. Yet, with his permission, I am writing from my slant as a child. From how I viewed life. My dad was much better at relating to Jan and me. And, in reality, who knows how we might have rebelled had we not been so traumatized by his behavior. It compelled us to goodness.

Those who plant in tears
*   will harvest with shouts of joy.*
They weep as they go to plant their seed
*   but they sing as they*
return with the harvest.
(Psalm 126:5–6)

Ten

My daddy was from the old world. Shouting and praying and pleading for the blood of Jesus. He would wring his hands and write checks to "My dear heavenly Father" for the church offering. He scrubbed his hands in the bathroom to wash the oil and crumbs from dinner . . . but also to cleanse the tiny kernels of sin that had probably gathered in his soul since the last meal.

His life showed an agitation, a

sensitivity. His hair grew thinner. He walked with a brisk, life-is-important kind of pace. And he prayed. *Not once, ever, did I hear my father speak a negative or unkind word about anyone.*

Daddy prayed for himself, mostly. For every atom of sin and self to be cleansed. I still don't know exactly what that means, but those were his specific words. He prayed for the atonement of the blood of Jesus to sanctify him. He would, right at the end of each prayer, pray for each of us. He prayed for every atom of sin and self in our lives. Then, later in life, each grandchild.

He prayed more for himself than for the lost world or those in the church. Probably he felt his condition was so degenerate that he could not move beyond that.

Daddy hugged us often, prayed constantly, and always worried. He preached that Jesus never failed, but he always seemed to be battling unknown forces. He insisted we see life his way—not because he was unkind, but because black and white gave him clarity.

For Fred, it boxed him in. He refused to
come inside the box because it suffocated
him. In my role of trying to keep everybody
happy, I continually worked at feeling safe
in the box, yet it was beyond my reach. *I
kept stepping out of the lines even when I did not
mean to.*

I am a mother of four boys and can
understand the frustration of kids arguing.
My father became very agitated . . . would
wring his hands . . . and remind us that this
broke God's heart.

But my mother would kiss our tears, remind
us that God has compassion, and that she got
frustrated too. She always diminished the
doom and condemnation and identified
herself with us. It gave us dignity.

Performance was in me from my earliest
beginnings. Performance equated acceptance
and approval from God. I longed for His
smile above all else.

My father was racked by inferiority too. I do
not say this because I want to cloud this

victorious life. He was unswerving . . .
absolutely unswerving in his love and
devotion to God. He never spoke unkindly.
NEVER! His love of his God and others
never varied. But Daddy never felt good
about himself.

He longed for more recognition. For a larger
church to pastor or a leadership position over
other pastors. He never felt he went very far,
but he wanted to be valued . . . and that
equated with position authority.

God knew no church could have a more
godly man. A prayer warrior . . . a gentler,
kinder man.

Harold Kiemel gave life and others his very
best, though it was not spectacular. Daddy
taught me there are levels of importance in the
world, and his striving bred the same in me.

What people did . . . their careers . . . titles . . .
achievements . . . were all significant to my
sweet father and mother. One's achievements
were always part of defining someone.
Though my parents never favored anyone,

degrees and titles and positions were
important to them.

I naturally grew up believing that
achievement would make me more
important. People would treasure me more.
Love me more for sure.

I would not trade my parents for anyone else.
I tear up often for they have crossed over to
glory, and I miss them so much. Daddy gave
me the drive and passion to love the world
for Jesus. Mother taught me style and grace.
She is the one who urged me to read all kinds
of creative articles for my writing acumen,
and the one who taught me an intimate
language that I use with my children today.
She bought me my first Anne Morrow
Lindburgh books.

In general, the soul makes progress
when it least thinks so. Most frequently
when it imagines that it is losing.
(Source unkown)

Eleven

I noticed everything. The way people looked at me. Whether anyone would smile or if they had a cautious slant as I walked by.

It was obvious that I was different. Blue-eyed. White. Tall and skinny.

The chocolate and caramel skins and the shimmering, shiny, black hair on all the moving bodies around me left me transfixed. How was it that some people could be so smiled upon by God? What had so many done to please God so?

My father would take us to call on a family . . . Oriental, naturally, for this was Hawaii. Quiet and sensitive, I would sit while my parents visited . . . and stare. The lovely skin. The crisp, starched blouse. The eyes so dark that they melted into a warmth that mesmerized me.

Maybe black children stare at white people. Maybe some of them long for fair complexions or light hair. I have often wondered. Do most children feel on the outside of the happy part of the world? Studying all the prettiness and glamour? Craving, like me, to be special?

At the beach, I was terrified of what everyone must be thinking of my body. At school, I knew others saw my loneliness.

I longed to keep Jan happy about having me as her best friend. And always, underlying every emotion I felt about myself, was the burning, raw understanding that I was not worth existence to Fred.

In the simplicity of my thoughts, I . . . without obvious choosing . . . willed myself to be smart. To achieve. To prove I was special.

It seemed to me that our lives revolved around Fred. He broke the rules. He resisted God (well, my father thought so). His anger and rage and defiance kept us in constant crisis. Today, I still do not understand it all. Always, the tears and terror hung around us as a thick shroud. I felt needy and always scared.

When someone smiled at me . . . across a counter in a store, or waiting on a street corner for the light to change, or in the elevator . . . I felt my heart swell. It felt kind. It gave me dignity.

The recess bell would ring. Third grade. Sixth. Ninth. The bell always told me one thing: I would be very lonely for fifteen minutes. Sometimes thirty minutes. Some recesses were shorter than others.

The feelings of inferiority were a daily occurrence. I assumed I was alone in these emotions. The beautiful and creamy brown-skinned students would never feel this way!

As I reflect, I can still feel those thoughts. Would someone be there to sit by me for lunch?

I was always on the honor roll without any effort, but I felt ugly and awkward and outside every circle.

Today, I know it built strength and character in me. Twenty-five years ago, I only knew I suffered.

I loved feeling loved. Kindness or a smile or a few, kind words meant everything! And, as an adult, I have always believed in those beautiful, small gestures, and strived to give back to others the loving gestures that were given to me.

Twelve

Mother was most people's ideal. She was beautiful. Her thick, coarse, luxuriant black hair was barely gray at sixty.

With large, liquid eyes . . . dark and expressive . . . she saw and enjoyed things that most of us miss. The skylines of large cities. Sitting in a car by the sidewalk and watching people—their differences, peculiarities, unique parts.

We watched very little television, but Mommy was crazy about raw talent. Geraldo Rivera as an investigative reporter. Shari Lewis and Lamb Chop. Sonny and Cher at the beginning.

Then there was her harmless love for rhythm. For jazz and "Tea for Two" along with the hymns. I think it came from a raw sense of intelligence and a yearning for self-expression.

She would serenade all those on the ocean liners we traveled on back and forth between the states and Hawaii. They loved her! My father always enjoyed this in my mother and never tried to stop her.

Whether she watercolored for us, or whipped up our favorite, homemade cake at night for bedtime . . . or bought fabric "at a great bargain" to make bedspreads or dresses . . . Ruth Geraldene Nash Kiemel looked at life as a magnificent gift. I literally cannot remember one single day in my life when Mother was unhappy. I am sure there must have been days, but I do not remember.

If Mommy had a downside, it was that she noticed everyone's external appearance. Maybe we all were concerned with that.

Mother always said it was Daddy and his prayers that would get us to heaven. He was the one who inspired dreams and a future. Mother gave me the only sense of safety in our tumultuous home. She never heaped guilt on herself or us.

My favorite part of life was every evening at our sit-down dinners. We loved what Mother cooked and that Daddy always let each of us talk about our day and listened with his enthusiastic interest.

I will give you a new heart with new and right desires, and I will put a new spirit in you. . . (Ezekiel 36:26–27)

Thirteen

Hawaii, 1963

Jan and I were juniors at McKinley High School, Honolulu, Hawaii. Four thousand island students . . . Japanese, Filipino, Chinese, Puerto Rican, and Hawaiian. At the very most, there might have been sixty Caucasians.

I dragged Jan into what I perceived was our sole opportunity for significance: song leading. If we could be elected, six or seven out of four thousand, and stand in front of bleachers at the football games, then our lives would not have been lived in vain.

Today, that logic is ludicrous to me, but at sixteen, it made perfect sense.

If we tried really hard . . . if we gave it all we had . . . we could win. Our lives would never again be lodged in obscurity. This was not just a way to significance. It felt like the *only* way. A do-or-die dilemma.

We practiced for weeks. Our muscles got so inflamed that we could not even move our legs for the student body tryouts. While everyone jumped and moved, we stood stiff, moving only our arms.

The first fifteen minutes of school, we went to homerooms for the Pledge of Allegiance and announcements over the intercom. Finally, the day after elections arrived, and the principal was going to read the winners "over the air."

Jan and I were in different homerooms. We never talked specifics, or in detail, about

much of anything. We shared a silent kind of
language, where we sensed each other's
emotions. We could not imagine winning.
Who knew us? Yet losing was unthinkable
too.

If we lost, the reality of our physical and
emotional existence would crumble before
us. It was sick thinking, yet real. Looking
back, we needed someone to prepare us for
the fate of losing.

As the names were announced, each
homeroom listened. There were claps and
cheers for those who won. I knew before the
last names were read because they were
presented in alphabetical order.

If someone had thrown me over a cliff or a
gushing waterfall, I would not have felt any
more finality. A silent force slugged me.
Knocking my senses askew. All my years . . .
those long, arduous paths . . . felt to no avail.

The long bus ride home, Jan and I were
silent and motionless. We could not even
instigate chatty banter or fake smiles. I felt as

if a skyscraper were leaning against my
chest, and I was fighting to even breathe.
With stoic containment, we endured until we
arrived at our bus stop.

A long, half block to home. We almost ran.
Without speaking to my mother, we headed
for our bedroom and threw ourselves across
our beds, sobbing. The pain started in our
toes, and tears from a deep cavern inside
found, at last, release. They had been bottled
tightly for so many years.

Finality clutched at our souls. There could be
no future. Only a million more days of quiet
desperation, eking out a survival of quiet
nothingness. Of insignificance. Of the world
dressed in glory and honor, marching past us.
Taunting us. Looking, condescendingly, at
our pathetic existence.

As children, our family unit was consumed
with my brother and father's ongoing
conflict. We never felt we were an integral
part. Combined with our twinhood, which
gave us even less individuality, we had never
found the "me" in each of us.

I had not considered life if we lost. There could be no future, could there? It took weeks, putting one foot in front of the other.

Amazingly, we learned life does go on. Time was salve on our wound. Food began to taste good again. Even, in time, we laughed again. In retrospect, I treasure that hard lesson. It helped me so much because it was real. Life is not a fairy tale for anyone. My children can know I was not born with success handed to me. And I empathize with their struggles. They are aware of which students are popular at their grade school. I see them looking for their own significance.

Even as I write this, the Winter Olympics in Nagano, Japan, are in progress. Many athletes, in multiple events, have spent their lives training to win the gold medal, or to place at all.

A poor landing . . . a fall . . . or a hundredth of a second behind across the finish line has been emotional for me to watch. Young adults who have poured years into rigorous training for one golden moment at the

Olympics . . . only to come up short. And
basically one effort away.

Significance defined by a win. A loss. A sense of
feeling loved and special and unique if you
win. But insignificant and unloved and a zero
if you do not. Allowing others to define one's
worth.

Brock, my beautiful, twelve-year-old son,
made the varsity wrestling team as a sixth
grader. He did very well until the last district
championship. Pinning his first opponent, he
moved up. In this match, the student keeping
score gave three points to the other wrestler
in error. After forty-five minutes of deep
discussion by his coaches with the umpire,
the points were left as they were. Brock was
out of the competition.

Trying not to cry . . . to not reveal emotion, I
sat next to him in the bleachers and
personally understood the devastation of
loss. Yet, life is not all winning. In fact, very
few truly great moments come along. I long
for my children to learn something I did not

for so many years. *That our beautiful uniqueness is created solely by God. No one, and no achievement, can define that.*

I spent most of my life allowing other, to dictate my worth, value, or shame. They told me if I was a good person by their words and actions. They defined me.

At times I still get my feelings hurt, or feel jealous. But I no longer allow others to hold my value and worth. Only God dictates that.

You will know the truth, and the truth will set you free.
(John 8:32)

Fourteen

Cedar Vista 1996

After my first week in Cedar Vista, Link Care, at Jan's urging, sent one of their psychiatrists to meet with me early each morning. A sense of such incredible loneliness, in the midst of acute suffering and fear, left me longing for a Christian comrade.

Cedar Vista's chemical dependency unit had a *spiritual* base. Not Christian, but spiritual. The AA program's

ultimate goal is to help those in recovery to
discover their "Higher Power." For anyone
with a serious addiction, AA believes there is
no hope for recovery within ourselves. "A
power greater than ourselves can and will
restore us to sanity if we ask . . ."

About 2 A.M., I huddled in the darkness . . .
chilled and miserable . . . in a chair on the
patio. A man in his seventies, alcoholic, walked
shakily out the door with a cigarette literally
dangling between his stained fingers. I was
praying . . . begging . . . God to hold on to me
until morning, and happy for any diversion.

This man had graduated from an Ivy League
university. Had worked in publishing, of all
things. As we visited, I asked if he had a
"Higher Power."

He was an atheist, he said. The only higher
power he considered was electricity.

The girl I became the closest to worshiped
the "goddess." My eyes began to bulge, and I
instantly, in my free-spirited way, told her
she needed Jesus. She lovingly reminded me

her road to recovery was different from mine.

Goddess? Electricity?! I was out of my element!

It was not that I felt judgment for anyone who did not believe as I did. I only felt scared and isolated. Having Larry, from Link Care, come each morning for fifteen minutes . . . and pray with me . . . fed comfort and strength to my bone-weary soul.

For Larry, I fear it was more challenging. I had never spoken an expletive in my entire life. Around AA tables, I was given a complete education on them.

Every morning, I had been through another ominous, wrenching night. Literally, *there were moments I believed I would disintegrate, and the nurse would find only a pile of ashes in my bed.* I felt my blood soaked the halls of Cedar Vista as I wrestled with the evil forces that were determined to enslave me. (The therapists would have told me this was "histrionic"!)

Histrionic behavior or not, my self-will was fighting against my battled, imprisoned soul. War it was!

In the tiny cubicle where Larry and I would meet, Larry listened to me. There were moments I screamed. Tears fell. And I even used a few expletives. Pain ripped through me, and it was Larry's job to help me hang on. Through it all, he never blinked an eye, and he was kind.

My journey was all-out warfare . . . between good and evil. Truth and contradiction. Purity and only the persona of purity. *The easy road fighting preeminence over the narrow, honorable path.*

I either had to defy all my learned behavior and with irrevocable iron will hold on until God led me out to a new place . . . or die.

For two weeks, I clung to the divine. I set my face like "flint." My nobility was nonexistent. God's love would not let me go. His love and grace wooed me and called me to freedom. Those days in Cedar Vista, I could not see

Him. Could not hear Him. But I knew Him. *He was the Healer. The Provider. The Restorer. My Rock.*

And I searched for Him. I humbled myself and, in some almost intangible way, I fought to find Him. And in finding Him, to embrace uncomplicated, untarnished truth. I would not relent.

As a mother trying to save her child. As a man crawling in some vast desert longing for water to quench his agonizing thirst. I longed for God. I was powerless. My life out of control. And He was the ONLY One who could bring me deliverance.

From the pain of my childhood, I moved forward, looking for clues from my adolescent and early adult years. In between therapy sessions and gym and all the activities that were to keep us moving in Cedar Vista, I would sit, close my eyes, and try to retrace my life steps.

I will go to the altar of God,
to God—the source of all my joy.
(Psalm 43:4)

Fifteen

Years ago, while at RAPHA, in Texas, I was asked by the spiritual counselor if I had a "hole" in me anywhere.

A hole? How did he know?! I had never told anyone. Yes, I did.

"Ann, if you have a hole, it means there is a crack in your soul!"

Without knowing how to define this, I was still riveted by the concept. It represented truth, though I was not able

to explain why. I did know I was broken.
Will and I had four babies at that point. Four,
miraculous, beautiful little boys from eight
months to four years of age.

As a child, so much of what I felt as a girl was
shaped by the only two men in my life: my
father and my brother.

My father loved me deeply, and it was his
passion for God and dreams that fueled mine.
Yet he battled so many of his own
incriminating feelings that I continually felt
inadequate to keep him happy; I felt inept
myself because he was, and he was my father.

Fred, my brother, obviously consumed with
his own internal battles for truth and
survival, unknowingly communicated
something that today he says was not real . . .
that he felt a sense of pathetic disgust for me.
Thus, I developed a longing . . . a thirst . . . to
be liked and approved of by men. Being an
identical twin added fuel to this because boys
would look at Jan and me as one entity
rather than two individuals. The privilege of

being unique did not exist through our
growing-up years.

Not once in summer camp did a guy hang out
with me or show the slightest interest. It cut
so deeply into my shame and sense of
rejection, yet I never told anyone. Not even
Jan. It was obvious to me that having a boy
actually like me was about as impossible as
the earth disintegrating. No boy would ever
find me appealing.

A very cute boy fell for Jan when we were
sixteen. I was elated. It was such a comfort
that *someone* liked Jan. I was not sad, but
hugely relieved.

As college freshmen, we attended a private
liberal arts school in Idaho. One of the most
handsome and sought-after senior basketball
stars came up to me in the student dining
hall and asked me out! Incredible! I was
stunned. He had been dating the most
popular senior girl from a wealthy family. I
was a lowly freshman. Suddenly, she was
jealous of me!

A college freshman at seventeen, I knew zero about dating . . . or men . . . and the interest he showed me was brief. For the first time in my life, I joined the ranks of all who are instantly infatuated and became a victim of the savage misery that comes when the dream bursts.

In some ways, I was ill with the desire to please. Ill with the longing to be accepted and embraced. Especially by men. *My ambitions soared out of my dual passions for God and for significance.*

When my early books became overnight best-sellers, and lots of men began to find me attractive, I was dismayed.

As I succeeded professionally, I was thrown into arenas in which I had no experience or preparation. The conflict between men wanting me sexually and my solemn commitment to purity became more and more an inferno inside my soul.

Through the days and nights in Cedar Vista, which melted into one long, nightmarish journey with no relief, I kept silently screaming for God. Begging Him to show mercy toward me. To peel the scales from my eyes. From my embattled, weary spirit. How had my soul been cracked? How?

With hesitation, in our therapy sessions, I cautiously began to address the men in my past. Not my father and brother, but the men, after college, who kept entrapping me . . . holding me captive. Taking away my freedom. Stealing my innocence and my rightfully deserved self-respect.

More important than anything, except my walk with God, was my commitment to sexual purity. In reality, one respected the other. It was a pledge I had made, very young, to God, to myself, and to the man I would someday marry.

Fresh out of college, I taught English and world history for two years and did some graduate work in journalism. From there, I moved to Long Beach, California, where I was hired full-time as the youth director of a large church.

Being very young and full of unrelenting
enthusiasm, I took on the world. Fearless.
Loving. For years, growing up, I listened to
my father weep and pray and love people.
The same compassion burned in me.

My assignment was to lead and guide all the
teens who attended this large, upper-middle-
class church. However, a man called one day
and asked if I would come see him. He said
he was lost and destitute. He had heard I
loved and cared about people like himself.
That was all I needed.

Looking back, driving to Hollywood . . . to a
rat-infested, old building . . . showed
unbelievable naïveté. Huge cockroaches
skittered here and there. All along the halls
were men in drunken stupors, and others using
drugs for some relief from their internal woes.
A creaky elevator barely made it to the top
floor. I found his room at the end of the hall
and knocked. I felt impenetrable. Protected.

The door opened. An unshaved, bedraggled
man stood in front of me. Eyes watering. He
had once been a handsome, brilliant,

successful man, with a gorgeous wife and two sons. He had once attended the church where I now worked. Alcoholic and pathetic, he asked if God could love him.

Could God love him? Oh, God loves EVERYBODY! Anywhere! No matter what!! My compassion for this broken man was huge. I prayed with him . . . that the God of the universe would heal his heart and give him a new beginning. There was a sense of excitement. Adventure. After all, was I not called to love and help lift others' burdens? I knew rejection and pain too well myself. Jesus lived for the sick and broken.

As weeks went by, I took some men from the church to see him. To encourage him. I was only twenty-two, and when he told me he was in love with me, I was horrified. I did not know how to say no. To help him understand that I was offering God's love, not my own. In his forties, he was old to me. I was suddenly stuck in a nightmare.

Here was a man . . . with incredible persuasion, convincing me I would fail God if

I did not marry him. Do as he said. And if I did not, I would not only disobey God, but he was going to kill himself. Genuine terror gripped me.

Often, he would come by my little studio apartment. He would reek with alcohol and, never having been around alcoholics, I was clueless. Cautiously confronting him, he would look aghast and say, "Of course, I am NOT drinking, Ann! I would never touch alcohol again. Don't you know that for months after you stop drinking alcohol, it seeps out of your pores?"

It felt questionable, but what did I know? I had lost the only "out" I could think of . . . that I could not marry a man who drank. In my thinking, I was stuck. My hopes and dreams for the future were instantly lost as I felt my mission was to forfeit everything to save this broken man. I drove through the streets, crying.

This was not a physical relationship. I remained very naive. Looking back, his intoxicated state was to my advantage.

The church had a governing board, and they were feeling concern for me. It had not crossed my mind to tell them of my plight. They brought me in. Said I would have to leave if I chose to marry Dick. I dissolved. When they assured me I was NOT responsible for this man's happiness, I felt I had been released from a literal prison.

Shortly after, I was offered a very exciting position as the youngest dean of women in America on a college campus. Bidding good-bye to several hundred teenagers I had grown to love deeply, I flew to Boston. Unsure. Scared. Inexperienced. Yet, with God in my heart, I was thrilled with a new assignment. And Boston! A place I had never lived before. I, again, was unprepared, but exhilarated!

History tends to repeat itself. One's thought processes, and the criteria by which decisions are made, often change very little, and we find ourselves in similar circumstances over and over and over again.

Going to Boston was exhilarating. I had been

invited to this college campus a short while
before where I was asked to be the keynote
speaker for the student body in its opening
week in September. It was one of those
electric experiences where students poured
in and we were all swept away by God's love.
Not something that often happened in the
staid, conservative community of East Coast
intellectualism.

Thus, I had some sense of my environment
where I would serve as dean of women. A
cute, small apartment was rented before I
arrived, and I bought a sports car to
commute.

I was not the typical dean. Young and
energized, I did what felt right, trying to
hang on to my individualism in an academic
atmosphere that could have intimidated me.
My boss was the most loved man on campus
and included me in coffee breaks with the
faculty.

My real stability those five years came from a
wonderful family that lived just blocks from
me. Dr. Calhoun was a professor at the

college, and his daughter, Susan, was a senior there. Norma Calhoun, his wife, prepared dinner every night at five o'clock, and I always had a place at the table if I could get there at that time. During my entire tenure there, I ate with this incredibly loving family, and Susan and I rode bikes, laughed, and were bonded for life. I will never forget their kindness and love. And I know God was a part of it because I would soon be entrapped again.

A professor from another New England university began dropping by our offices. Incredibly handsome and impeccably dressed, he subtly began to woo me. He complimented me on how I looked, my intelligence, and the "creative" innovation I brought to this staid office.

At first he would always invite other administrators to join him and me for lunch. I loved the sense of belonging and the prestige I felt in those moments. Once in a while, I would be invited to his home for dinner. His wife was very sweet, almost sensitive to her lack of college education, but warm and loving, and I really enjoyed her. They had four children.

This family lived relatively close to the university where I worked, so it did not seem unusual for this man to be seen on campus.

As the months rolled by I felt more and more relaxed in my position. I was twenty-four; I had never had a serious relationship with any man. This may seem strange but I was never "boy crazy" and found myself detached at times.

It became an incredible compliment that this highly successful man seemed smitten by me. Initially I felt he admired me simply as a college dean, but more and more he began to voice his unhappiness in his marriage. That he was unloved and unappreciated. Lonely and filled with despair. Yet how strong and dignified he felt around me. I . . . who had steadfastly believed I was defective . . . and this sophisticated man was drooling over me!

It was very difficult and confusing. I loved his wife and children and became a quasi-

confidante to him. Because he called himself
a *Christian* . . . attended church regularly with
his family . . . and was very loved and
respected by my boss and others, I assured
myself that mutual respect was harmless.

Barely escaping the last man who would kill
himself without me, I was quickly being
locked into the same mentality with this
man. Only this time, he was far more shrewd
and calculating, and I was too naive to
recognize it.

At this time, my identical twin was getting
married. We all loved Tom. Incredibly
handsome, extensively educated, and
accomplished, I was thrilled that Jan, who
looked just like me, had won a man of his
caliber. Maybe we were not so pathetic!

However, Jan was my dearest friend and
confidante in the world. I felt even more
vulnerable.

In truth, I did not want a sexual relationship.
An affair. I wanted marriage. A family. And
regardless of whether his marriage was on

the rocks or not, I could not have taken a
man from his wife. Even if he divorced her.
All of it . . . any of it . . . was diabolically
opposed to my personal, Christian beliefs
and my integrity.

It took a lot of time for this man to delude my
thinking, but I longed for intimacy . . .
affirmation.

Worst of all, I felt I could tell no one. It
would betray this man, who was highly
respected in the New England area and by
my boss. Who would understand? Believe
me? What would Jan say? I had never kept a
secret from her, but I felt secrecy was
demanded.

The white became gray. The obvious
completely confused. Truth was no longer
truth as I understood it. I knew what the
Bible said about adultery and men loving
their wives. All my life, I had lived it and
breathed it. Yet, in an incredible, unbelievable
way, I became completely lost. Blind. This
man said God's plan for us was different!

Many nights in the next two-and-a-half
years, I would crawl into my sports car
where no one could hear me. Driving up and
down streets, I would literally scream and
moan and sob with despair. Filled . . .
consumed . . . with contradictions. I begged
God, over and over, to show me truth.

This man said nothing so beautiful could be
wrong. That I was a gift from God. God was
in this.

At twenty-seven, I lost my virginity to this
married man. I vacillated from "How can this
be?" to "How can it not be?"

His words, "I cannot live without you!"
haunted me. His wife confided in me that he
drank. But, of course, he had serious heart
problems, she said. His children loved me. I
feared I might go mad. Yet in my own lost
way, with Jan married, I talked myself into
love, for I so wanted it. I felt so alone. *But, in
exchange for love, I had to relinquish freedom.*
That beautiful, clean, unashamed gift of
looking ANYONE in the eye without fear or

shame or incrimination. No secrets. Nothing to hide.

To not be free. To live a lie. To pretend one thing when you are really something else. The terror that boiled deep in me that I would be found out. Rejection. An outcast. Who would understand that this man knew exceptions that God allowed?

And even worse, always loving truth and now not even knowing what it was.

I often boarded a plane to speak somewhere. Thousands would come, standing ovations. Then I would return to hotel rooms, falling facedown on worn carpets, and weep tears shed from an imprisoned heart that held no hope of a way out. I longed to walk away, but how? In my mind, I was again trapped. Smothered. Pinned against the wall of hopelessness. Someone's suicide on my hands.

Could I get another job in a faraway city? At this point, I had two books . . . numbers one and two on the top ten best-seller list. In both books, I wrote what I truly believed and the

ways I tried to love. My lie was in what I did
not say. There could not have been a
punishment more brutal than the agony of
enslavement.

Investigating several new job opportunities, I
hoped and prayed, but nothing panned out.
Trapped, with another man threatening
suicide daily if I left.

Everything was out of focus for me except
one: I could not marry a man who left his
wife. It seems ludicrous that, knowing this, I
continued in this secret relationship. But
everything was so out of focus. That is,
except that one, totally unblurred truth when
it came to his wife.

This highly educated Christian man felt no
shame. He never seemed to feel there was a
double standard. And as I began to claw my
way out of this nightmare, this man became
more and more physically and verbally
abusive.

This is not about victimization. It is about my
shame base before I ever got to Long Beach

or Boston. About my insatiable need to feel loved and accepted and significant. About the unhealthiness in me that forced me to keep others happy at the risk of totally blotting out my own sense of well-being no matter what damage it did to me. My own safety. My own health. My own peace and joy.

Even as I write this, I cry. The pain I endured. The insanity. It defined so much of my life. It stifled my marriage. Today, I know I must respect myself enough to really love anyone else. I must take care of me in order to care for you.

One day, as I was longing to extricate myself from the sick entanglement, this man called and asked me to meet him at an airport hotel. After arriving at his room, he began to slap me. Slug me. I was terrified, literally, for my life. Fleeing to the bathroom and locking the door, I shook with fear for two hours and when I heard him leave, I fled.

One morning very early, working in my office, he came by and asked to talk. As I calmly told him of my continuing decision to

back away, he got up and again began to slap
me against the wall.

On my own, with only God Himself as my
confidant, I backed away more and more. He
would call late at night and tell me he was on
a ledge somewhere. Ready to jump. It
sounds simple enough to say this was
ultimate manipulation. But being entrenched
in codependency and addicted to
performance and praise, I assure you it was
the hardest thing I had ever done. *God did not
take me out of the nightmare, but delivered me . . .
empowered me . . . in the midst of it.* He did not
fail me. I had screamed and begged for truth,
and I began to understand how entrenched
denial can be. How subtly the "angel of
light" had blinded me.

God revealed the truth because I believe He
knew my heart. He brought me out of chilled
darkness and lies to the fresh joy of truth. He
forgave me; washed my soul with the
radiance of His light.

Nonetheless, the experience led me into
other abusive situations with men that took

me several years to overcome. My addiction to perform and my terror of rejection kept me consenting to things I did not feel good about. Things that only increased my shame and self-loathing.

There were other men whom I wanted to lead to Jesus, yet found them trying to lure me to their idea of love. I was starved for men to like me, yet surrendering to any of their antics never enhanced my self-worth or dignity and only shredded the respect I had.

What devastated me the most were men who claimed to live by an honorable, Christian standard, but wanted out of me what I felt I could not give.

All I had ever really wanted was a husband and children. I had waited. And then I met Will. Will was thirty-seven and a virgin. He had saved himself all those years for me. Will knew my past, but he believed I was God's woman, and he loved me.

We were excited. Happy. Our families totally supported us. We did not announce our wedding plans until we had given God a month to give us any no's.

People flew in from across the globe. The wedding was beautiful and special. And we flew off to a glamorous honeymoon.

*Unless the LORD builds the house,
 the work of the builders is useless. . .
 (Psalm 127:1)*

Sixteen

Idaho Falls, Idaho, July 1981

Will and I moved into a brand-new, very lovely home. We had all the appearances of love and joy and success and glamour.

Yet, the hole in my soul, shaped at a very early age, spoke darkness and fear and insignificance to my very being. This reality began to explode in me, and I found it less and less possible to push it under. To ignore it.

The pressure and stress began to break down my immune system.

Living twenty-four hours a day with a man who was as stubborn and strong-willed as I was. He saw life in black-and-white. Most of the time, I could not.

Will wanted me to cook and clean and budget groceries in a manner most proficient to his way of doing things. I had my own style. We wanted babies as soon as it could happen. A big mistake. Before we could even learn to know each other, we were consumed by what we might be able to create. I so wanted to please. So longed for children. But not enough to eat and do all Will thought it would take to be successful at it. I could not handle his attempt to control me.

I was a bride in a small community, far from anyone I knew except Will. It was so scary. Different. And I started having miscarriages and physical problems. The stress and the resentment that came from a growing confusion of who I really was attacked my body. With each miscarriage, I felt more disappointment, shame, and sadness.

All my life, I had worked so hard to prove to

everyone that I was smart and kind and
strong. Now, I could not even carry a baby.
The sense of defectiveness consumed me.

When the doctor gave me my first morphine
shot, at thirty-five years of age, for the pain
from a raging abdominal infection, I was
amazed. Having been a purist all my life, and
never even considering pain medicine, I was
shocked at how wonderfully that morphine
blocked the pain.

What I did not know was that morphine not
only took my physical pain, it gave me a
sense of well-being. It numbed the anguish of
inadequacy and failure to perform.

After marriage, when I could not perform in
the only thing I had ever dreamed about and
longed for—making babies—my stamina to
keep smiling, no matter what, was gone. I
had been a full-blown addict of performance
and praise since childhood. I was an addict of
pain pills, just waiting to happen.

The shots and pills mellowed me out. Made
me feel peaceful even when almost nothing

was going right. When Will got angry and upset with me . . . or I with him . . . I popped a pain pill and quickly felt better. Sometimes even euphoric. What I did not understand was the reality that a body builds tolerance to anything after a while. As a child, a dentist always had to give me one or two extra shots to numb my gums. When I had surgeries, after marriage, to clean out scar tissue or to treat an abscess from a miscarriage, I was informed every single time that at 5'8" and 112 pounds, they nearly had to kill me to knock me out.

My metabolism is extremely fast. Most normal doses of antibiotics do not work on me. So, as I began to take more and more pain pills, my body became resistant. It took several years for this to happen, but at some point there was no more euphoria. It was just taking what I needed for pain or to keep me from withdrawal. I could no longer sleep without medicine or go to the grocery store without some in my purse.

God gave us four extraordinary, beautiful boys. I wrote and spoke. We traveled worldwide. Yet I was not at peace. The self-

loathing and incrimination remained. The
conflicts between Will and me coninued.

Being the nurturer . . . having been
programmed all my life to please . . . left me
vulnerable. With a family, friends, fans—I
gave and gave. All the while, I was growing
more and more resentful under the surface.
It was give, give, and give some more. There
was not enough coming in to nurture me.

My children were so much more beautiful
and dear to me than I could ever have
imagined. But all the joy they brought me did
not help me quit pain pills or like myself
better. Now, I had to be a great mother. The
children must look perfect, for we were a
family par excellence!

The hole got deeper. Expectations I kept
heaping upon myself . . . thinking to be loved
and popular I had to now appear a perfect
wife and mother. Try. Try. Try.

Day Nine—Cedar Vista—3 A.M.

That hole in me . . . the rage that I DENIED

existed in me began to seep through more and more. My cranky roommate was snoring.

I felt half crazy. Stark-raving mad. On the floor. Face buried in my hands. My spirit screamed out. Silent tears falling. *Relentlessly, I wrestled with God.*

No! I could not go on without some relief. Some assurance that I was not pounding the doors of heaven in vain. I could not! The very powers of darkness made me feel their fingers were clinging to me, refusing to let the sickness leave me.

Something happened that chilled, dark summer morning. Something profound. The "hole" left me. The gaping, aching vacuum was gone. The evil was dispelled. The crack sealed. I have not felt it since. And every single day, I thank God. Every day, I now taste the freedom that had eluded me so many, many years.

Love never gives up, never loses faith, is always hopeful, and endures through every circumstance.

(1 Corinthians 13:7)

Seventeen

I walked out of the doors of Cedar Vista after twenty-five days. No longer barred from the outside world. No longer protected from the influences that could undo all that had been accomplished.

Scared. Excited. Fearful. Relieved. Many mixed emotions. The air smelled so fresh. The sky so blue. The flowers so lush. Now, I could put to the test all I had learned during those anguishing group therapy sessions.

Still incredibly thin and weak, and my
entire body raw with pain, I felt very
fragile. I had not seen the apartment that
Jan had found for the boys and me to live
in. Had never resided in this area, so I knew
nothing about the streets or how to find my
way around.

Filing separation from Will was devastating
for me and for him. He remained in Chicago,
where he had a small company. The children
and I settled here.

We knew no one. The boys had not been to
school but had been privately tutored in
Chicago. I felt they needed to be placed in a
public school, and all but Taylor were very
excited. They did very well.

Learning to pay my own bills, feed the
children, be responsible for the discipline and
the healing that needed to take place in their
lives. There were many moments of terror
and fear.

Jan flew on to meet Tom on a business trip
the day before I was released. She felt we

would all do better if we started out by
ourselves. It felt right.

To try and define all Jan did while I was in
the hospital would be impossible. She
became my hero. The children adored her.
She let Colson and Brandt snuggle on each
side of her every night. She kept them safe
and content in a way that no one else could
have. When I was in Cedar Vista, the raging
inferno of withdrawal and infection and
mental, physical, and emotional duress were
beyond anything I could have imagined.
Knowing the children were happy fueled my
courage and allowed me to face what I
needed to. I truly believe I would have
cracked and folded without knowing the
children were happy and safe.

Pledging to attend ninety AA meetings in
ninety days was a huge undertaking. It
meant I had to leave the children daily.
Colson cried every single time, and I would
cry most of the way to the meeting because it
broke my heart. God helped me do ninety
meetings the first ninety days, and ninety the
second ninety days. If, to remain "clean,"

someone told me I had to stand on my head
at every meeting, I would have. Period.
Some of the most courageous people I have
ever met have been around Alcoholics
Anonymous tables.

Every Tuesday night for fifteen months, I
attended "Aftercare," a two-hour group
therapy session with others who had been
through Cedar Vista. It was, without
exception, the most difficult experience of
those fifteen months. Confrontation.
Confession. Exposure of our fears and
stumblings. Somehow, as when I was in-
house there, I seemed to get more mileage
from everyone than any of the others. I
would go in, praying to be ignored, and get
blasted time and time again. It *never* got easy.

One night, a recovering addict-alcoholic
confronted me. "Ann, I do not know who you
are. The way you talk . . . I always feel as if
you are standing behind a podium or a
microphone . . . etc."

My face burned red-hot. Shame.

Humiliation. Georgette, the therapist, said, "Ann, how does that make you feel?"

"I want to say, 'I hate you, Laura' . . . ," I blurted out, in tears.

Crawling into bed late that night, I could not sleep. My emotions swirling. At 1 A.M., I went to the phone and called Laura.

"Laura, sorry to call so late. Please tell me what you were really saying in group. What do I say and do that makes you feel as you do? I so want to grow!"

Laura and I have been very good friends since. I learned and grew because of her sincere honesty.

Every Tuesday night, I braced myself. No matter how terrified I was to discuss something going on in my life, I relentlessly handed it to the group. There was no turning back. I could NOT build a safe wall around me, for I had done that all my life. It had pulled me into drowning waters.

One Tuesday night a month was "family" night. The children were so sweet, but they never wanted to go.

"Mom, you go work with your alcoholic friends," Colson said. "We know you like them!"

But I dragged them there. They had seen me on pills and sleeping as much as I could. With Will working all the time on new ventures and me sleeping so much, they had to fend for themselves far more than they should have. They were children. I not only took them to the family group sessions but took them to private therapy with me for several weeks. They were darling. Winsome. People were continually captured by their sweetness.

To be a woman and not a child. To learn to find peace in what God thinks instead of what everyone else does. To live with highs and lows and have to feel the anxiety on both ends of the spectrum. To parent the children with maturity. To stand through the pain and feel it all.

In many ways, I was a kid at heart. Bike rides. Ice-cream cones. Laughter and play. The children and I had always had so much fun because I loved kid stuff. Now I was becoming, internally, a woman. How does a woman parent? It was trial and error.

We were in a pet store one day. Puppies. We had never had a dog because our lives were always in turmoil and we traveled so much.

"Mommy, can we have that puppy? Please? Please? Pretty please?"

I succumbed. An apartment. Four little boys. And now a puppy. Totally outside my comfort zone. What does anyone do with a puppy that poops on the carpet and yelps and howls whenever you leave?

This was a mistake. My sensible boundaries had been overstepped. With the children in tears, I quietly talked to them all the way back to the pet store five days later.

"I was wrong to buy this puppy. Without question, I understand your longing for a puppy. Daddy and I want you to have one, but this is not the time. . . ." Basically, I had presented it this way: "Do you want a puppy or a mom?"

A puppy or me. How could they argue? We handed the puppy over with my assuring the children a special, loving family would take it . . . and came home with a kitty. In my mind, I reasoned that children need something like that to love on.

This kitty was neurotic. We were not sure she had a functioning brain. If she saw fish in a fish tank, she would run and hide rather than watch them or try to get to them.

Yes, we had goldfish too. Then the cat had kittens (what do I know about such matters?). Now we have the mother cat, pregnant again.

We had two rabbits. As anyone can already see, I can be talked into a lot. If nothing else, the boys have learned to take care of all these creatures, and they have added fun for us. I am also learning to say "no" more often.

Will and I never learned to appreciate each other's gifts and talents. Will had all his own ideas about how I should run the house. Cook. Clean. For me, I felt he was a drill sergeant and made demands that were far too heavy on the children and me.

A year apart, we each began to understand how much we needed the other's strengths and gifts. Children need structure. They feel safe in it. It was very hard not having Will to help.

My sensitivity and heart made the children feel safe. They confided in me about everything, such as if some kid at school was mean to them or they felt insecure. Will saw how they loved me, and that regimen without some individual empowerment was unhealthy.

Children need a mother and a father. They also need to hear parents admit when they have been wrong. Will and I are philosophically so different. We have opposite approaches to just about everything. But the year apart really changed us. We began to learn new ways to communicate. A new language.

Our dear friends, Herb and Dona, stood by all of us. They paid the rent and made the car payments. Will's money each week covered groceries and all the expenses of living. Money was tight, and to stretch it was one of the most scary, difficult assignments as single mom. There were days I did not know how we would eat. And there were so many "overdrawn" notices the first few months I became nearly paralyzed before opening the mailbox. Many kind people were there to see us through.

Steve, a banker, began to help me balance my accounts. Bonnie and Mary tutored Colson and Brandt in reading for free. Carl and Jill brought money over so the boys could each buy some books at the book fair. Marian and Joan handed me cash to help at Christmas.

I came to Fresno knowing, literally, no one. God placed such beautiful people in our path. My children went to a terrific grade school close by. There were moments I feared the principal would think the Andersons were taking over.

Some children in Colson's class came to school with lice in their hair. When the school nurse called me asking that I come pick Colson up, I was horrified. Lice?

I scrubbed his head. Sprayed the furniture. Washed sheets and towels. At moments I felt my own head itch. Paranoid, I feared lice would take over our lives. I stopped by the doctor's office, whispering to the receptionist that my children might have lice. Could the doctor check all our heads?

At Christmas, the school nurse arranged groceries and gifts to be brought in. All my life I had been a giver. It was a humbling challenge to be needy and receive. But God gave us, daily, everything we needed.

For the first time, I was introduced to Moms In Touch. Had never even heard of the group previously. Christian mothers praying together for our children. It was the most significant thing I did every week for my children. I heard other mothers cry over their children . . . and listened as they wept and prayed for mine. I was riveted with love and hope. This year, Taylor is in seventh grade so I attend two Moms In Touch a week. I see God answer prayer.

Will came for Thanksgiving. Two great families (their children attended where mine did) had us over for a feast we will never forget. There was such love. Such kindness. After dinner, Will took us to San Francisco for the weekend. Caution. Some apprehension. All the issues that needed to be worked on. Will and me. Will and the children. But we had a really special time.

All my life, I had never had the strength to take care of me. Nor the courage to be honest. I had spent my life crying for everyone else's sadness, never believing myself deserving of such. To say to Will, "I need a year to face my own issues. A year in personal recovery. My prayer is that you will spend the year addressing your family of origin and conflicts," took a maturity I had never understood before. Seeing the

pain in Will . . . his sadness was
devastating. Yet I believed, in the deepest
parts of me, if we did not allow God to
destroy the warps and cracks and self-
willed ridges in our old foundations . . . and
help us build a new, solid base, we would
ultimately not make it.

It meant so much to me that Will had Bill
Gothard and some other dear families from
Bill's Institute to support him. No one has
been kinder than Bill to our family. We all
love him profoundly.

Public school is an experience that creates its
own dynamics. Let's start with secular
children's verbiage. My children had never
been exposed to such. Sheltered and guarded
and home-schooled (believe me, I was a
brain-damaged home schooler!), the boys
were very protected. Will and I felt positive
about that.

Yet, I felt . . . with my own limitations . . . that
they needed a dose of the real world. Of
proving God faithful there and anywhere. Of

being with other children and facing the
unique challenges that regular school
brought. I had been through public school, as
had Will, and I was practical enough to think
it healthy.

When Will and I moved to Chicago, our
family was in jeopardy. Will had a major
project in Russia and was traveling back and
forth. Never learning to feel my gut and
honor the truth that reverberated from it, I,
again, was thrown into despair. Others
continued to define what I needed to be.
How I ought to think.

Home-schooling and other ideological
preferences were not what I felt comfortable
with, yet, feeling powerless, I continued to
compromise my instincts to keep others happy.

Now, in California, I had to find my way
back to some middle ground of conscience. It
was not easy. Suddenly, I was solely
responsible for all my own actions, and I was
not sure what I felt about some issues. There
were times, in my search, that I leaned too far
one way or the other. Somehow, I felt love

from God . . . compassion . . . in the midst of
my wanderings.

Between the expletives I heard daily and the
language the children heard at school, we
were quite a group. There were boundaries,
naturally. Most of what the children brought
home in their verbiage was harmless. I would
roll my eyes, smile, and go on. Some
expressions, though, were simply,
unequivocally, not allowed.

Some days, I would be driving somewhere . . .
errands or sports events . . . and one of the
children would look over at me and ask if
they could say a bad word. "Mom, please . . ."

With the boundaries established, I nodded
and allowed some independent expression
for our ears only. They loved it!

Several times, I flew east. Meeting publishers
and having speaking appearances allowed me
the opportunity to spend a couple of days
with Will, now and then.

This was an incredibly painful time for both

of us. Will felt his world had disintegrated, and I, in an unswerving determination, felt time was our most healing asset. Time to reflect. To dig deeper. To allow God to be our mate. To draw strength from Him. There were so many things that I had never felt worthy enough to own with Will. Experiences that hurt me deeply. I became a river of emotions and questions.

With amazing seduction and subtlety, I had sold the basic core of who I was down the river and had tried to embrace all that others thought I should be. I had totally lost my way.

When I saw Will in such pain, I was melted. Often, long-distance, I would sing old hymns of the church to him. In every way I could, I strived to be gentle and kind. Yet never once, that I recall, did I do that at the sacrifice of my own well-being.

Living in an apartment with four children was a fresh adventure. Somehow our apartment became the center of activity for all those in the complex. I became mom, referee, prayer warrior, and snack cook. Almost all the children came from divorced parents, with mothers working to put bread on the table. Every Sunday, we squeezed as many as we could in our car and took them with us to church.

Of course, it seemed complaints came frequently. My children were too noisy. They bounced their basketball too early for an older woman who wanted to sleep until ten. Could my children be more subdued in the swimming pool? Brandt left his bicycle on the sidewalk. Did I not know one of my children was going to get hit by a car, rollerblading so much? Quit snapping those popguns. They are dangerous.

The first year, I felt I had to apologize to the whole world for having four sweet-spirited-but-active boys.

Things that did not come easy for me, I still attempted. Giving the children chores to do, especially on Saturdays. Putting one to bed early because of a bad attitude. Helping at school.

Never have I felt more vulnerable than when watching my children compete at sports and struggle to find their niches at school. Quickly, I realized that it was hard for me not to over-identify with my children in areas of their pain. I kept working on all these issues, even though some days I felt I was sliding backward half the time.

One of my very best friends was Catherine. She had a mother's heart so similar to mine. I could call her in tears over a bad day one of my children had, and she would cry too. I will never forget!

God gave our family a wonderful church, Clovis Hills Community. The senior pastor, Steve, was a tremendous help to me the first year before Will came, and after, when the two of us were in counseling with him.

Two years ago I would stand in front of the mirror many times. I no longer recognized the face I saw. Often, I would think that if I could get a face lift . . . anything of improvement externally . . . I would become happy. My shame and self-loathing had never dissipated. It only became more aggressive in the tearing down of my morale.

My body looked like a teenager's, but my face appeared dull and tired. Old! For years, I felt if we could just move somewhere else, life would be better. If I were not so pathetic in my appearance, I would be transformed into a joyful human being.

What I failed to understand was this: *Wherever I went, I had to take myself along.* The same inferiorities and sick coping skills. Thus, God did for me what I could not grasp for myself.

He forced me into a difficult, narrow, and trepidating journey to my heart. For a full year God had me spend all my energy facing myself. Dealing with confusions and improper values that lived in the very essence of me. I was forced to stand, naked and exposed, again and again as others confronted my inconsistencies and double standards.

In Cedar Vista, I typically felt I was unique. My background, my life history, somehow

was a cut above or beyond anyone else's.
Believe me, they set me straight. I came to
realize that all of us grapple with the same
tough conflicts. Our similarities always
outdid our differences. I was no more special
or victimized than anyone else. It was a hard
pill to swallow when I had to confront the
fact that my addictions were MINE. And
they were not invented by Will Anderson. He
had his issues that had seriously damaged our
relationship, but the addictions and
codependency were the sick things I alone
brought to the table.

Will came again for New Year's. With each
visit, healing took place. Grievances, even by
the children, were voiced. Forgiveness
granted, again and again. As a child, my
mother used to say this: "When people are
unhappy with each other . . . each side
defensive and blaming the other . . . it is like a
big cauldron. There is confusion. Mistruths.
Half-truths. Only time can define reality. In
time, the truth always rises to the top."

Will had his version of our problems. I had
mine. But as days and months went by, we

each began to see ourselves and each other in a different light. School was going to be out, and I planned to move back to the Chicago area, closer to Will, where we could look at *our* issues. It had been a long year.

During my time in Cedar Vista, I learned some invaluable lessons about the road to recovery. More than any was the counsel to change NOTHING my first year.

In 1996, when I flew to California with the boys, there was no time frame. Frankly, I was totally clueless about what the problems were . . . aside from Will Anderson. The longer I searched within me, the more I found to confront. And I was repeatedly advised that if I could succeed through my first year of recovery, my chances of continued healing were far greater. Very few get to the second year.

I was challenged to get phone numbers from those I met around AA tables, so in a time of frustration and temptation, I could pick up the phone and get help.

Probably the most significant learning block
I was given was the challenge to keep
stepping back from situations and quietly
give things a second look.

When someone upset me . . . or I was
provoked, rather than get totally bent out of
shape, I observed myself. Confronted the
point that so jabbed at me. Not always, but
often, I realized the conflict said more about
me than anyone.

In the Tuesday night aftercare, I often was
in tears because I felt someone did not like
me. It was such a raw feeling . . . allowing
myself to stand still and absorb the
rejection. To experience it rather than
instantly move into my "be so nice they have
to like you" mode. Or instantly start finding
fault so that the pain was shifted to them
instead of toward me.

One afternoon, I called Georgette, a
therapist I loved. A recovering addict herself,
she took special interest in my children and
me. "Georgette, I'm so sad. Last night, before
our group session, Lori said there are some

people she just does not care for. I was one of them. It hurts so much!"

Georgette responded, "Ann, is Lori really someone you want to be close to?"

Stopped. Stunned. Well, not really. Lori and I had little in common. I simply felt if she didn't like me, some dark shadow was carved into my core worth. I realized no one can steal my worth.

One day, I called to see my internist. My thyroid medication was gone, and I needed a new prescription. Years before, following so many miscarriages, I developed Hashimoto's Disease and needed thyroid supplements. But three of my children were home with some flu bug, and I decided to take two of them with me so the doctor could check them. My money was very tight, and I decided to kill three birds with one stone, so to speak.

He was gracious. Wrote out my prescription. Listened to Brandt's and Colson's chests. As I stood to leave, I mentioned Taylor, who I felt needed some medication to clear up a few adolescent pimples. My doctor looked at me. "Ann, today I am only seeing those who are very sick. You will have to set up another appointment for that."

My heart stopped. The blood rushed to my face. Stammering a quick thank-you, with shame I exited the medical building.

It hurt so much. I had overstepped my boundaries. Offended him. He did not like me. Was exasperated. I was a bad person. And I could not undo it. That guttural shame was what forced me, in years past, to perform. Or, for comfort, to pop a couple of pain pills.

As I stoically drove home with my two sons, I began to pray that God would simply help me to process this pain. That I could not undo it but wanted wisdom to process it.

Within minutes, peace came to me. I found myself saying, "Okay. I inappropriately overstepped my boundaries. I am human. I fail. So?! Lee, my doctor, is not going to wipe me off his roster of patients for that. This is a learning experience."

On and on, I began, with health, to look at a bigger picture. Let the failure go.

This may seem very overdone and foolish, but for me, it was an amazing leap toward health. Similar scenarios will probably happen on and off the rest of my life, and I pray for God to continue gracing my life with truth and maturity.

I will never fail you.
I will never forsake you.
(Hebrews 13:5)

Eighteen

Clovis, California, July 1996

It had been less than two weeks since I walked out the door of Cedar Vista. Still struggling to sleep at night, I was doing my best to care for the children . . . attend AA meetings . . . and stabilize physically. My body still ached and hurt inside and out.

One morning, Taylor came into my bedroom. "Mom, I feel real sick. My stomach hurts . . ."

"Oh, darling, I am sorry. Is it nausea or cramps or what?"

"Cramps . . ."

Taylor has always been stoic about pain. Too stoic, I have often felt. When he was small, a bee stung him. A tear or two came to his eyes, but that was all. Often, I encouraged him to let his feelings come through.

"Taylor, do you need to go to the bathroom?"

"I don't know . . ."

"Try, darling. I have an AA meeting to run to. I will be back in an hour . . ."

When I returned home, he was curled in a ball. His sweet face showed pain. Filling the tub with very warm water, I helped him get in. The warmth seemed to help him. We did this several times that day. I even gave him a little laxative pill, thinking that was still probably the problem.

Several times, he threw up. He followed me

around the apartment, curling up by me. I was so new to the area and did not have a physician. I basically knew no one. Surely this was the flu?

Close to 5 P.M., I became rather alarmed. Taylor was lying in a heap by my bed. Again, he began vomiting, and I ran for a towel. Picking up the phone I called Pastor Steve at Clovis Hills Community Church. I still barely knew him, but wondered if a doctor attended church there that I might call?

Steve could not think of anyone specifically. Hanging up, I began to pray. "Jesus, I feel so alone. This worries me. Please show me where I should turn . . ."

Within moments, the phone rang. It was a doctor. Though he had never been by the church office, he had just walked in, and Steve asked him to call.

Does Jesus care? Always. Yes, He is the Father to the fatherless. The husband to the wife. Rapha . . . the Healer. Restorer. A present help in the time of need.

"Ann, this is Edgar Vera. I am a doctor. Can I help you?"

Carefully, I began to give him Taylor's symptoms. Abdominal pain. Some nausea and vomiting.

"Have Taylor roll over on his back. Ask him to show you where, specifically, his pain is."

Suddenly, Taylor was pointing to the lower right side of his abdomen.

"Ann, take him to the emergency room immediately. It sounds like Taylor has appendicitis!"

Appendicitis?! It had never occurred to me. I broke into tears. What if this was true? All day, I had allowed him to suffer. Given him a laxative. What kind of a mother was I?!

Leaving eleven-year-old Brock to watch Colson and Brandt, I headed out the door with Taylor. He looked so miserable. So sick.

Drawing his blood and taking his temperature confirmed Edgar's diagnosis. Elevated white count. Fever. I was called to the phone.

"Ann, this is Edgar. Here are a couple of names of terrific surgeons. Both Christians, and very qualified! My wife, Brenda, and I are praying for you. We have enjoyed your books!"

> God answers prayer in the morning
> God answers prayer at noon
> God answers prayer in the evening
> So keep your heart in tune

Steve's wife, Shirley, came to the hospital to be with me when they rolled Taylor into the operating room at 2 A.M. So thoughtful. I called Will in Chicago and had someone spend the night with my three children at home.

Dr. Jackson did the surgery. An incredibly kind and sensitive man. When they rolled Taylor out, he opened his eyes and said, "Hi, Mom. . . . They showed me my appendix . . ."

The surgery had gone well. Taylor's appendix had been very enlarged. When I was a junior in college, I had an appendectomy, but, for some reason, I assumed this rarely happened to children. Especially a child barely twelve years old.

For two-and-a-half days, I lived in this semiprivate hospital room with Taylor. They gave him morphine through his IV for thirty-six hours. Such a challenge, for I was in early recovery from pain medicine, and morphine had been one of my "drugs of choice." My favorite, in fact!

The entire time, I had nurses bring me every chocolate pudding on the floor. Exhausted, miserably scrunched in a hospital chair . . . I ate to calm my agitation. For the first time in my life, I gained weight. Over the next few months, I put on twenty pounds.

Though I needed to gain some weight, this scared me. I found myself eating a lot of ice cream. Frankly, a lot of everything. Twenty pounds was more than I felt good about.

We were taught at Cedar Vista that every day was a victory if we remained alcohol- and drug-free. Gaining weight? The IRS after us? Denting the car fender? Take one day at a time. Not yesterday or tomorrow. Simply today. And God . . . or one's "Higher Power" . . . will take care of the rest.

Amazingly, I not only gained more weight than I liked, I did scrape the fender of our leased car backing out of the narrow garage. I had woes about bills. Watched the children wrestle through some of their own anger as a result of Will and me not being where we should have been.

Will was still in Chicago. He was running a small company. In Cedar Vista, the therapists emphasized over and over that for one year we should NOT change *anything* in our lives.

I had come to California with the boys and had filed for separation before going in to Cedar Vista. Thus I committed to a full year away from Will . . . in California . . . to face the complexities of my own internal issues.

Will wanted us to return home. However, those closest to the situation also felt Will's and my issues were complex and needed space and time to resolve. As I groped for answers about myself, I prayed Will was doing the same.

God definitely had our attention, and with the distance between us we could not point at each other. We had to look inward.

One day, I was struggling. I did not like my body. And couldn't the bank show some mercy toward me?! A dear friend, calling long-distance, told me (rather harshly, I felt), "Go back to your husband!"

In tears, I knelt and pleaded with God to sustain me. Almost immediately I remembered a song by Bill and Gloria Gaither that I had always loved.

> Yesterday's gone . . . and tomorrow may never be . . . but we have this moment today.

Love washed over me. The sweet smiles of

my children's faces. Azure blue skies. The
sun on my skin. Health, that for so many
years had been mine . . . then was lost . . . was
returning.

> Strength for today and bright hopes
> for tomorrow . . .

Today, as I reflect, I smile. Taylor is strong,
with only a small, noble scar. I lost the weight
eleven or twelve months later. As I gained
internal strength and growing serenity, the
need to fill the once-gaping hole was no
longer there. The fender is fixed, and I have
learned much about budgeting, paying bills
on time, and carefully planning ahead.

God never transforms all the struggle and
pain into glorious victory and sunrise
overnight. At least He never has with me.
But in time . . . one day at a time . . . with
obedience and trust . . . He evolves, through
process, incredible tomorrows of joy and
growth and surprise and blessing.

Majestic strength comes when God leads us through
self-willed valleys . . . and sets us free. A purging

*wrought out of a complete letting go. The wounds
He allows do not last forever. In total surrender, the
miracles do come. The sunrises do sweep across our
petulant darkness. We do laugh again. God
promises!*

We ask God to give you a complete
understanding of what he wants to do
in your lives . . . that you will be
strengthened with his glorious power . . .
May be filled with joy
(Colossians 1:9, 11)

Nineteen

*H*erb and Dona, the couple who really dug deep for a year to help us financially and otherwise, were faithful in their prayers and love for us.

On an overseas flight, they sat across the aisle from another couple . . . George and Colleen Jackson. While casually chatting, the man told Herb they lived twenty minutes out of Fresno. Fresno?!!

George Jackson had a large operation in Kingsburg, California. I had not even heard of Kingsburg. He grew gourmet fruits. He had just completed a state-of-the-art packing plant, and needed help. Herb immediately thought of Will.

Herb and Dona, on their private jet, stopped in Chicago and picked Will up. They were flying to Fresno. We all met George and Colleen, and miraculously, Will was offered a place in the company.

The children and I were ecstatic. We loved California. The dry air. Mild winters. We would not need to move.

God allowed me the privilege to sign two new book contracts, and Will and I and the boys began a healing process. Weekends, all summer, going to the mountain lakes to fish and boat and water-ski. School reconvening, and Will and I trying to test the waters of two parents working together with the children's homework and other points of conflict.

For eight more months beyond the first year,
Will and I met with our pastor frequently.
We shared moments of intense frustration.
Forging our way through the opposing
convictions and preferences. The children
working to articulate some of their own
struggles and feelings.

During this entire time, Will and I did not
have a physical relationship. Instead, we
focused on intimacy that revolved around
vulnerable sharing. Around unforgettable
outings with the children. Around honest
struggles and how we each felt about our
sixteen years of sexual oneness. We married
after knowing each other only six months —
and long-distance at that.

Spiritual and emotional oneness took more
and more work . . . struggling to expose our
hidden fears and longings.

As a woman, I longed for us to be kindred
spirits. For so many years, I participated in
sexual intimacy with Will even when I was
angry and resentful and felt alienated. I did

not want to fail God or Will, but it was not honest and not healthy. This time around we refused to take shortcuts, but at moments it was frustrating.

The end of January, I flew to Nashville for the presentation of my first new book in five years, *This Is a Story About God*.

I contacted my four beautiful birth mothers, inviting them to spend the weekend with me in Nashville.

It had been nine years since we had all been together. Beth, my youngest son's birth mother, was eight months pregnant with Brandt in 1988, when I introduced her to our other three birth mothers while speaking in Birmingham. Now I wanted to fill the birth mothers in on all the victories that had been won in our lives since.

Our time in Nashville was magical. Dick and Dodie Pridgen, Colson's maternal grandparents, fed us. Kept a roaring fire. We basked in the love of a magnificent Lord. In our love for the children. For each other. The pitfalls we have all been through. And thoughts of the future. It was a beautiful, rich time.

Life has been hard.
We lost our way.
Though we entered into marriage with
sincerest love and commitment,
we were not prepared
for how difficult marriage can be.
But God has smiled on us.

Please join
Will and Ann Anderson
and the children
as we repeat our vows . . .
as we take all the lessons
God has taught us the last two
years . . . and start afresh.

March 22, 1998, 4:30 P.M.
At the home of
George and Colleen Jackson

Dinner Following.

Twenty

Kingsburg, California March 22, 1998

The day streamed with sunshine and held a vast, cloudless sky. With spring flowers bursting everywhere, some of our closest friends gathered at George and Colleen Jackson's elegant and tucked-away country home.

Down a tree-shaded drive, in the quietness of a late Sunday afternoon, Will and I rededicated ourselves to each other and God after twenty-two months of separation.

Even as we had married on a Sunday afternoon, so we chose another Sunday to start over. It had been a long and arduous journey.

The children, dressed in khakis and polo shirts like their daddy, were a significant part of the ceremony too. Will and I each spoke to them. Spoke of our failures, and pledged to them our love for each other and our commitment to allow God to make our family what He desires.

Will surprised them with new pocketknives. He said boys can never have too many!

I looked into my children's eyes, sparkling with innocence and untarnished love and hope. I spoke of my love for their daddy and my earnest desire to be a mother who knows peace and tranquillity. My gift was large jawbreakers from their favorite candy store.

Will and the boys unwrapped a beautiful gold chain with a cross and hooked it around my neck.

Everyone shared in Communion, and then we celebrated in an elegant, sit-down dinner and "roast"! The Jacksons, as hosts, outdid themselves. Everything was exquisite, and none of us who were there will ever forget or be the same.

Shirley and Danae Dobson flew in with Herb and Dona. Others came from far away. After kissing our children good-bye and leaving them in the care of Summer, a darling twenty one year old, we joined Shirley and the Fishers. Flying on their jet to Colorado Springs and the Broadmoor Hotel, our favorite place. Massages and getting our hair done and laughter and love.

Jim and Shirley and the Fishers joined us in the Penrose Dining Room, at the Broadmoor, for dinner Monday night. Love and jokes and great food and camaraderie. Our closest friends had stood by us through so much!

And God's love covered us. All of us celebrating the matchless grace and miraculous mercy that heal broken hearts. That transform a union once angry and bitter and destructive into one of bonded tenderness.

Over the years, *many* gave input to Will and me. Herb and Dona invested money, and hours and hours in long-distance phone calls. Sweat and devotion and prayer that consumed their lives for a year. They obeyed God. Completed their mission. And all they poured into us was blessed by God. He smiled on His work through them to us.

I was more shy and nervous to crawl into bed with Will after twenty-two months of separation than I was on my wedding night sixteen years before. And when it was time to fly back home I was apprehensive to walk back into our home. How would the children do? Had we changed enough? Was God big enough to continue the transformation process?

But my fears were unfounded. Will and I are

changed. Everything is different. I have
never known such gratitude and joy and
peace. The children are happy. They appear
secure. Grateful. I revel every day in this
fresh, clean vibrance that covers us.

*Will and I will always have differences, but when we
find ourselves going toward our old behavior we are
catching ourselves.* Stopping. Taking a step
back. Being quiet. Handing our conflict to
God and finding middle ground. For us,
marriage will always take work, but we are
not afraid. Our respect for each other is such
a rich, new emotion.

It will take sacrifice, hard work, and time to
dig ourselves out of the financial hole we are
in. We did not get here overnight, thus we
will not crawl out overnight. Yet, we have
learned so much. We are committed to the
journey toward financial freedom as another
part of our family's need to be free.

Conclusion

Today my worth is no longer defined by what others think. My value and self-respect come from the glorious Lord who created me.

There are still moments when I feel scared, fearing that I might recede into total obscurity, and never be loved or respected again. Today, I know that to dissolve this anxiety I must discover ways to give myself away. To let go of the focus on myself and do beautiful things for others through God's power. I go to

God and in His name to others. This is the ultimate source of all my joy and significance.

Will and I cannot undo the failures of the past, but we are working, with God's help, to change what we can.

Our children are imperfect and human, but miraculously remain sweet and uncomplicated in their love and optimism.

In June, as I was going over the final changes to this manuscript, our family was again jarred with bad news. What we thought was a kidney stone in Will has been diagnosed as a malignant tumor in his left kidney. Cancer. Typically, for those in grief, we began with denial. How could this be?! Joy, excitement, and new beginnings have been dashed with one harsh diagnosis.

Today we know one thing for sure: God is sovereign. He is good. He sees the big picture and never makes mistakes. Through the pain, miracles are born. Strength and security come. We will wait and trust.

I no longer need pills to dull the pain. No matter what the blows of life bring, I know who my anchor is. That is enough.

> At the Cross
> At the Cross
> Where I first saw the light
> And the burden of my heart rolled
>   away
> It was there by faith
> I received my sight
> And now I am happy all the day.

This is after all a story of redemption. A journey to the heart . . . led by God . . . to set me free. My chains are gone. My soul has taken flight. I am redeemed.

How I celebrate. I love to watch the very presence and Life of God wash across my once dark and confused heart . . . shedding warmth and deliverance. Alleluia, Alleluia, Amen.